COMPREHENSIVE GUIDE TO FOREX AND CRYPTOCURRENCY TRADING

Introduction

What is Forex Trading?

Foreign exchange (Forex or FX) trading involves the exchange of one currency for another on a decentralized global market. It is one of the largest and most liquid markets in the world, operating 24 hours a day, five days a week. Participants include banks, financial institutions, corporations, governments, and individual traders.

What is Cryptocurrency Trading?

Cryptocurrency trading involves buying, selling, and exchanging cryptocurrencies like Bitcoin, Ethereum, and others on various digital asset exchanges. Cryptocurrencies are decentralized digital assets based on blockchain technology, and their market operates 24/7 globally.

Part 1: Understanding Forex Trading

Chapter 1: The Basics of Forex Trading

1.1 What is Forex?

- Definition of Forex
- History of Forex markets
- Importance of Forex trading

1.2 How Forex Trading Works

- Currency pairs (e.g., EUR/USD, GBP/JPY)
- Exchange rates
- Bid and ask prices
- Pips and pipettes
- Lots (standard, mini, micro)

1.3 Major Forex Markets

- The major trading sessions (London, New York, Tokyo, Sydney)
- Overlapping trading sessions
- Market participants

Chapter 2: Fundamental Analysis in Forex

2.1 Economic Indicators

- GDP
- Unemployment rates
- Inflation rates
- Interest rates

2.2 Central Banks and Monetary Policy

- Role of central banks
- Monetary policy tools (interest rates, quantitative easing)
- Impact on currency value

2.3 Political and Geopolitical Factors

- Political stability
- Trade agreements
- Geopolitical events

Chapter 3: Technical Analysis in Forex

3.1 Chart Types and Time Frames

- Line charts
- Bar charts
- Candlestick charts
- Time frames (minute, hourly, daily, weekly)

3.2 Technical Indicators

- Moving averages
- Relative Strength Index (RSI)
- Bollinger Bands
- Fibonacci retracement

3.3 Chart Patterns

- Head and shoulders
- Double tops and bottoms
- Triangles
- Flags and pennants

Chapter 4: Trading Strategies in Forex

4.1 Day Trading

- Scalping
- Intraday strategies

4.2 Swing Trading

- Identifying trends
- Using support and resistance levels

4.3 Position Trading

- Long-term trends
- Fundamental analysis integration

4.4 Risk Management

- Setting stop-loss orders
- Position sizing
- Diversification

Chapter 5: Forex Trading Platforms and Tools

5.1 Choosing a Forex Broker

- Regulation and security
- Trading fees and spreads
- Leverage and margin requirements

5.2 Trading Platforms

- MetaTrader 4 and 5
- TradingView
- Broker-specific platforms

5.3 Using Trading Tools

- Economic calendars
- News feeds
- Analytical tools

Part 2: Understanding Cryptocurrency Trading

Chapter 6: The Basics of Cryptocurrency Trading

6.1 What are Cryptocurrencies?

- Definition of cryptocurrencies
- Brief history (Bitcoin and altcoins)
- Blockchain technology

6.2 How Cryptocurrency Trading Works

- Cryptocurrency exchanges
- Trading pairs (BTC/USD, ETH/BTC)
- Market orders and limit orders
- Liquidity and volatility

6.3 Major Cryptocurrencies

- Bitcoin (BTC)
- Ethereum (ETH)
- Ripple (XRP)
- Litecoin (LTC)

Chapter 7: Fundamental Analysis in Cryptocurrency

7.1 Evaluating Cryptocurrencies

- Whitepapers
- Development teams
- Use cases and adoption

7.2 Market Sentiment

- Media influence
- Social media and forums
- Market psychology

7.3 Regulatory Environment

- Government regulations
- Legal status of cryptocurrencies
- Impact on the market

Chapter 8: Technical Analysis in Cryptocurrency

8.1 Chart Types and Time Frames

- Similarities with Forex charting
- Unique aspects of crypto charts

8.2 Technical Indicators

- Moving averages
- RSI and MACD
- Volume analysis

8.3 Chart Patterns

- Similarities with Forex patterns
- Unique crypto patterns

Chapter 9: Trading Strategies in Cryptocurrency

9.1 Day Trading

- Scalping in crypto
- Intraday strategies

9.2 Swing Trading

- Identifying trends in crypto
- Using support and resistance levels

9.3 Long-term Investing (HODLing)

- Buy and hold strategy
- Identifying strong projects

9.4 Risk Management

- Setting stop-loss orders
- Position sizing
- Diversification in crypto

Chapter 10: Cryptocurrency Trading Platforms and Tools

10.1 Choosing a Crypto Exchange

- Security and regulation
- Trading fees and spreads
- Supported cryptocurrencies

10.2 Trading Platforms

- Binance
- Coinbase
- Kraken
- Decentralized exchanges (DEXs)

10.3 Using Trading Tools

- Crypto news aggregators
- Portfolio trackers
- Analytical tools

Part 3: Advanced Topics in Forex and Cryptocurrency Trading

Chapter 11: Algorithmic Trading

11.1 Introduction to Algorithmic Trading

- Definition and benefits
- Types of algorithms

11.2 Developing Trading Algorithms

- Programming languages (Python, C++)
- Backtesting and optimization

11.3 Implementing and Managing Algorithms

- Choosing a platform
- Monitoring and adjusting algorithms

Chapter 12: Trading Psychology

12.1 Understanding Trading Psychology

- Emotions in trading
- Common psychological pitfalls

12.2 Developing a Trading Mindset

- Discipline and patience
- Managing stress and emotions

12.3 Building a Trading Plan

- Setting goals
- Creating a strategy
- Sticking to the plan

Chapter 13: Risk Management and Trading Discipline

13.1 Importance of Risk Management

- Protecting capital
- Consistency in trading

13.2 Risk Management Techniques

- Position sizing
- Diversification
- Using stop-loss orders

13.3 Maintaining Trading Discipline

- Following the trading plan
- Avoiding impulsive decisions

Conclusion

Final Thoughts

- The importance of continuous learning
- Staying updated with market developments
- Adapting to changing market conditions

Resources for Further Learning

- Recommended books
- Online courses and webinars
- Trading communities and forums

Appendices

Glossary of Terms

- Key Forex and cryptocurrency terms

Useful Tools and Resources

- List of helpful websites and tools for traders

Sample Trading Plans

- Examples of Forex and cryptocurrency trading plans

Chapter 1: The Basics of Forex Trading

1.1 What is Forex?

Definition of Forex

Forex, short for foreign exchange, refers to the global marketplace for buying and selling currencies. It is the largest and most liquid financial market in the world, with a daily trading volume exceeding $6 trillion. Unlike stock markets, Forex operates 24 hours a day, five days a week, across major financial centers worldwide.

The Forex market allows participants to trade currency pairs, such as EUR/USD (Euro/US Dollar) or GBP/JPY (British Pound/Japanese Yen). The price of each pair represents the exchange rate between the two currencies, indicating how much of the quote currency (the second currency in the pair) is needed to buy one unit of the base currency (the first currency in the pair).

History of Forex Markets

The history of the Forex market can be traced back to ancient times when merchants exchanged goods for other goods or currencies. However, the modern Forex market has evolved significantly over the centuries:

1. **Gold Standard (1870s - 1914):** The gold standard era saw currencies backed by physical gold reserves. This system provided stability in international trade but limited monetary policy flexibility.
2. **Bretton Woods Agreement (1944 - 1971):** Post-World War II, the Bretton Woods Agreement established fixed exchange rates pegged to the US Dollar, which was convertible to gold. This system aimed to provide economic stability and prevent competitive devaluations.
3. **End of Bretton Woods and the Free-Floating System (1971 - Present):** In 1971, the US abandoned the gold standard, leading to the collapse of the Bretton Woods system. Currencies began to float freely, with their values determined by supply and demand in the market. This marked the beginning of the modern Forex market.
4. **Technological Advancements and Globalization (1990s - Present):** The rise of the internet and advancements in technology have revolutionized Forex trading. Online trading platforms and electronic trading systems have made Forex accessible to individual traders and investors worldwide.

Importance of Forex Trading

Forex trading plays a crucial role in the global economy for several reasons:

1. **Facilitating International Trade and Investment:** Forex allows businesses and investors to convert one currency into another, enabling cross-border transactions. This is essential for international trade, investment, and tourism.

2. **Market Liquidity and Efficiency:** The immense size and liquidity of the Forex market ensure that currency prices are highly responsive to economic events and news. This contributes to efficient price discovery and reduces the cost of currency exchange.
3. **Economic Indicators and Policy:** Currency exchange rates reflect the relative health of economies. Central banks and policymakers monitor Forex markets to assess economic conditions and implement monetary policies. Forex trading can influence interest rates, inflation, and overall economic stability.
4. **Investment Opportunities:** Forex trading offers a wide range of opportunities for traders and investors. With leverage, margin trading, and various trading strategies, participants can profit from currency fluctuations. The market's round-the-clock operation also allows for flexible trading hours.

In summary, Forex is a dynamic and vital component of the global financial system, enabling international trade, influencing economic policies, and providing opportunities for traders and investors worldwide.

1.2 How Forex Trading Works

Currency Pairs

In Forex trading, currencies are traded in pairs, known as currency pairs. Each pair consists of two currencies: the base currency and the quote currency.

- **Base Currency:** The first currency in the pair (e.g., EUR in EUR/USD).
- **Quote Currency:** The second currency in the pair (e.g., USD in EUR/USD).

The value of a currency pair represents how much of the quote currency is needed to buy one unit of the base currency. For instance, if EUR/USD is 1.1200, it means 1 Euro is equivalent to 1.12 US Dollars.

Examples of Currency Pairs:

- **EUR/USD (Euro/US Dollar):** Represents how many US Dollars one Euro can buy.
- **GBP/JPY (British Pound/Japanese Yen):** Represents how many Japanese Yen one British Pound can buy.
- **USD/JPY (US Dollar/Japanese Yen):** Represents how many Japanese Yen one US Dollar can buy.
- **AUD/USD (Australian Dollar/US Dollar):** Represents how many US Dollars one Australian Dollar can buy.

Currency pairs can be categorized into three types:

1. **Major Pairs:** These pairs involve the most traded currencies and usually include the US Dollar. Examples: EUR/USD, USD/JPY, GBP/USD, USD/CHF.

2. **Minor Pairs:** These pairs do not include the US Dollar but involve other major currencies. Examples: EUR/GBP, EUR/JPY, GBP/JPY.
3. **Exotic Pairs:** These pairs include one major currency and one from a smaller or emerging market. Examples: USD/TRY (US Dollar/Turkish Lira), USD/ZAR (US Dollar/South African Rand).

Exchange Rates

An exchange rate is the price of one currency in terms of another currency. Exchange rates fluctuate constantly due to supply and demand dynamics in the market. Factors influencing exchange rates include economic indicators, interest rates, geopolitical events, and market sentiment.

For example, if the exchange rate for EUR/USD is 1.1200, it means 1 Euro is worth 1.12 US Dollars. If the exchange rate changes to 1.1300, it means the Euro has strengthened against the US Dollar, or the US Dollar has weakened against the Euro.

Bid and Ask Prices

In Forex trading, the **bid price** and the **ask price** represent the prices at which a currency pair can be bought or sold.

- **Bid Price:** The price at which the market (or your broker) is willing to buy the base currency in exchange for the quote currency. It is the price you will receive when you sell the currency pair.
- **Ask Price:** The price at which the market (or your broker) is willing to sell the base currency in exchange for the quote currency. It is the price you will pay when you buy the currency pair.

The difference between the bid price and the ask price is known as the **spread**. For example, if the bid price for EUR/USD is 1.1200 and the ask price is 1.1203, the spread is 3 pips.

Pips and Pipettes

A **pip** (percentage in point) is the smallest unit of price movement in Forex trading, typically representing a one-digit move in the fourth decimal place of a currency pair. For example, if EUR/USD moves from 1.1200 to 1.1201, it has moved by 1 pip.

Some currency pairs, particularly those involving the Japanese Yen, are quoted to two decimal places. For example, if USD/JPY moves from 110.50 to 110.51, it has moved by 1 pip.

A **pipette** is a fractional pip, representing a one-digit move in the fifth decimal place. For example, if EUR/USD moves from 1.12000 to 1.12001, it has moved by 1 pipette.

Lots (Standard, Mini, Micro)

In Forex trading, currencies are traded in units called lots. A lot represents a standardized quantity of the base currency.

- **Standard Lot:** A standard lot is 100,000 units of the base currency. For example, if you buy 1 standard lot of EUR/USD, you are buying 100,000 Euros.
- **Mini Lot:** A mini lot is 10,000 units of the base currency. For example, if you buy 1 mini lot of EUR/USD, you are buying 10,000 Euros.
- **Micro Lot:** A micro lot is 1,000 units of the base currency. For example, if you buy 1 micro lot of EUR/USD, you are buying 1,000 Euros.

Trading in different lot sizes allows traders to manage their risk and exposure more effectively. For example, beginner traders might start with micro or mini lots to limit potential losses while they learn the market.

In summary, understanding how Forex trading works involves grasping the concepts of currency pairs, exchange rates, bid and ask prices, pips and pipettes, and different lot sizes. Mastering these basics is crucial for navigating the Forex market successfully.

1.3 Major Forex Markets

The Major Trading Sessions

Forex trading is a 24-hour market, thanks to the presence of different global trading sessions. These sessions correspond to the opening and closing times of financial centers around the world. The four major trading sessions are:

1. **Sydney Session**
   - **Hours:** 10:00 PM - 7:00 AM GMT
   - **Characteristics:** The Sydney session is relatively calm compared to other sessions. It is the first session to open after the weekend, and trading volume starts to pick up.
2. **Tokyo Session**
   - **Hours:** 12:00 AM - 9:00 AM GMT
   - **Characteristics:** The Tokyo session is also known as the Asian session. During this session, currency pairs involving the Japanese Yen (JPY), such as USD/JPY, EUR/JPY, and GBP/JPY, experience higher volatility and liquidity.
3. **London Session**
   - **Hours:** 8:00 AM - 5:00 PM GMT
   - **Characteristics:** The London session is the most active trading session. The European markets are open, and there is significant trading activity in pairs involving the Euro (EUR), British Pound (GBP), and Swiss Franc (CHF). This

session overlaps with both the Tokyo and New York sessions, leading to increased liquidity and volatility.
4. **New York Session**
   - **Hours:** 1:00 PM - 10:00 PM GMT
   - **Characteristics:** The New York session is the second most active session. It overlaps with the London session, resulting in high trading volume and volatility. Major currency pairs, including EUR/USD, GBP/USD, and USD/CHF, are heavily traded during this time.

Overlapping Trading Sessions

The most active and liquid times in the Forex market occur during the overlapping trading sessions. These overlaps provide increased trading volume and volatility, which can create more trading opportunities. The key overlapping sessions are:

1. **Tokyo-London Overlap**
   - **Hours:** 8:00 AM - 9:00 AM GMT
   - **Characteristics:** This overlap is relatively short and less significant compared to the London-New York overlap. However, it can still offer good trading opportunities, especially for currency pairs involving the Japanese Yen.
2. **London-New York Overlap**
   - **Hours:** 1:00 PM - 5:00 PM GMT
   - **Characteristics:** This is the most significant overlap, as it involves two of the largest financial centers in the world. The increased trading volume and volatility during this time provide ample opportunities for traders. Major currency pairs, including EUR/USD, GBP/USD, and USD/CHF, experience heightened activity.

Market Participants

The Forex market consists of various participants, each with different roles and motivations. The main market participants include:

1. **Central Banks**
   - **Role:** Central banks, such as the Federal Reserve (Fed) and the European Central Bank (ECB), play a crucial role in the Forex market. They manage their respective countries' monetary policies, influence interest rates, and intervene in the currency markets to stabilize their national currencies.
2. **Commercial Banks**
   - **Role:** Commercial banks are the largest players in the Forex market. They facilitate currency transactions for clients, including businesses and governments. They also engage in proprietary trading, where they trade currencies for their profit.
3. **Financial Institutions**
   - **Role:** Financial institutions, such as hedge funds, pension funds, and investment firms, participate in the Forex market for investment and speculative purposes.

They often engage in large-scale trading activities and can influence market movements.

4. **Corporations**
   - **Role:** Multinational corporations participate in the Forex market to facilitate international trade and investment. They need to exchange currencies to pay for goods and services, manage foreign exchange risk, and repatriate profits from overseas operations.

5. **Retail Traders**
   - **Role:** Individual retail traders participate in the Forex market through online trading platforms provided by brokers. They trade currencies for speculative purposes, seeking to profit from fluctuations in exchange rates. Retail trading has grown significantly in recent years due to advances in technology and accessibility.

6. **Brokers and Market Makers**
   - **Role:** Brokers act as intermediaries between retail traders and the interbank market. They provide trading platforms and access to liquidity. Market makers, on the other hand, provide liquidity by quoting both bid and ask prices for currency pairs, enabling traders to buy and sell currencies.

7. **Governments**
   - **Role:** Governments participate in the Forex market to manage their foreign exchange reserves, stabilize their national currencies, and influence economic policies. They may intervene in the market by buying or selling currencies.

In summary, the Forex market operates 24 hours a day, with major trading sessions in Sydney, Tokyo, London, and New York. Overlapping sessions, particularly the London-New York overlap, offer increased trading opportunities due to higher liquidity and volatility. The market is comprised of various participants, including central banks, commercial banks, financial institutions, corporations, retail traders, brokers, market makers, and governments, each playing a crucial role in the functioning and dynamics of the market.

Chapter 2: Fundamental Analysis in Forex

2.1 Economic Indicators

Economic indicators are vital statistics about an economy's performance and are crucial for Forex traders to understand the health and direction of an economy. These indicators can significantly impact currency values. Key economic indicators include GDP, unemployment rates, inflation rates, and interest rates.

GDP (Gross Domestic Product)

Definition:

- GDP measures the total value of all goods and services produced within a country over a specific period, usually quarterly or annually.

Importance:

- GDP is a primary indicator of an economy's health and growth. Higher GDP growth typically indicates a strong economy, which can lead to a stronger currency as investors seek out higher returns.

Impact on Currency:

- Positive GDP growth can strengthen a country's currency as it attracts foreign investment. Conversely, negative GDP growth can weaken a currency due to reduced investor confidence and economic prospects.

Unemployment Rates

Definition:

- The unemployment rate is the percentage of the labor force that is unemployed and actively seeking employment.

Importance:

- The unemployment rate is a critical indicator of economic health. High unemployment suggests economic distress, while low unemployment indicates economic stability and growth.

Impact on Currency:

- Lower unemployment rates generally strengthen a currency as they signal a robust economy. Higher unemployment rates can weaken a currency due to potential declines in consumer spending and economic growth.

Inflation Rates

Definition:

- Inflation measures the rate at which the general level of prices for goods and services rises, leading to a decrease in purchasing power.

Importance:

- Moderate inflation is normal in a growing economy. However, high inflation can erode purchasing power, while deflation (negative inflation) can indicate economic problems.

Impact on Currency:

- High inflation can weaken a currency as it reduces purchasing power and may lead to higher interest rates to combat inflation. Conversely, low or stable inflation can strengthen a currency as it maintains purchasing power and economic stability.

Interest Rates

Definition:

- Interest rates are the cost of borrowing money, set by central banks. They influence economic activity by affecting consumer spending, business investment, and inflation.

Importance:

- Interest rates are a primary tool for central banks to control inflation and stabilize the economy.

Impact on Currency:

- Higher interest rates can attract foreign investment, strengthening a currency. Lower interest rates can weaken a currency as they make investments less attractive to foreign investors.

2.2 Central Banks and Monetary Policy

Central banks play a crucial role in managing a country's monetary policy, influencing economic stability and currency value.

Role of Central Banks

Definition:

- Central banks are national institutions responsible for managing a country's currency, money supply, and interest rates. Examples include the Federal Reserve (Fed) in the United States, the European Central Bank (ECB), and the Bank of Japan (BOJ).

Functions:

- Central banks implement monetary policy, maintain financial stability, and regulate financial institutions.

Monetary Policy Tools

Central banks use various tools to achieve their economic objectives. The two primary tools are interest rates and quantitative easing.

Interest Rates:

- Central banks set benchmark interest rates, influencing borrowing costs, consumer spending, and investment.
- Raising interest rates can slow down an overheated economy and control inflation.
- Lowering interest rates can stimulate economic growth by making borrowing cheaper.

Quantitative Easing (QE):

- QE is a non-traditional monetary policy tool where central banks purchase government securities or other financial assets to increase the money supply and encourage lending and investment.
- QE can lower interest rates and increase liquidity in the financial system.

Impact on Currency Value:

- Monetary policy decisions can have a significant impact on currency value. For example, a central bank raising interest rates to combat inflation can strengthen the currency as higher rates attract foreign investment.
- Conversely, implementing QE or lowering interest rates can weaken a currency due to increased money supply and lower returns on investments.

2.3 Political and Geopolitical Factors

Political and geopolitical events can greatly influence currency values and market sentiment.

Political Stability

Definition:

- Political stability refers to the degree to which a government is stable and its policies are predictable.

Impact on Currency:

- Stable political environments attract foreign investment, strengthening the currency. Political instability, such as government corruption, protests, or frequent changes in leadership, can weaken a currency due to increased risk and uncertainty.

Trade Agreements

Definition:

- Trade agreements are treaties between two or more countries to facilitate trade by reducing tariffs, quotas, and other barriers.

Impact on Currency:

- Positive trade agreements can strengthen a currency by boosting economic growth, increasing exports, and attracting foreign investment.
- Conversely, trade disputes or the imposition of tariffs can weaken a currency by reducing trade volumes and economic growth prospects.

Geopolitical Events

Definition:

- Geopolitical events include international conflicts, wars, natural disasters, and other significant occurrences that can impact global stability.

Impact on Currency:

- Geopolitical events can cause uncertainty and volatility in the Forex market. For example, a war or natural disaster can weaken a currency by disrupting economic activity and increasing risk aversion among investors.
- In contrast, resolutions to conflicts or successful management of crises can strengthen a currency by restoring confidence and stability.

In summary, fundamental analysis in Forex involves understanding and interpreting various economic indicators, central bank policies, and political and geopolitical factors. These elements collectively influence currency values and market dynamics, providing traders with the insights needed to make informed trading decisions.

Chapter 3: Technical Analysis in Forex

3.1 Chart Types and Time Frames

Technical analysis in Forex trading relies heavily on charts to visualize and analyze market movements. There are different types of charts and various time frames traders use to make informed decisions.

Chart Types

Line Charts:

- **Description:** Line charts connect a series of data points with a continuous line, typically showing the closing prices of a currency pair over a specific period.
- **Usage:** Line charts are useful for identifying overall trends and long-term price movements but provide limited information on price fluctuations within the trading period.

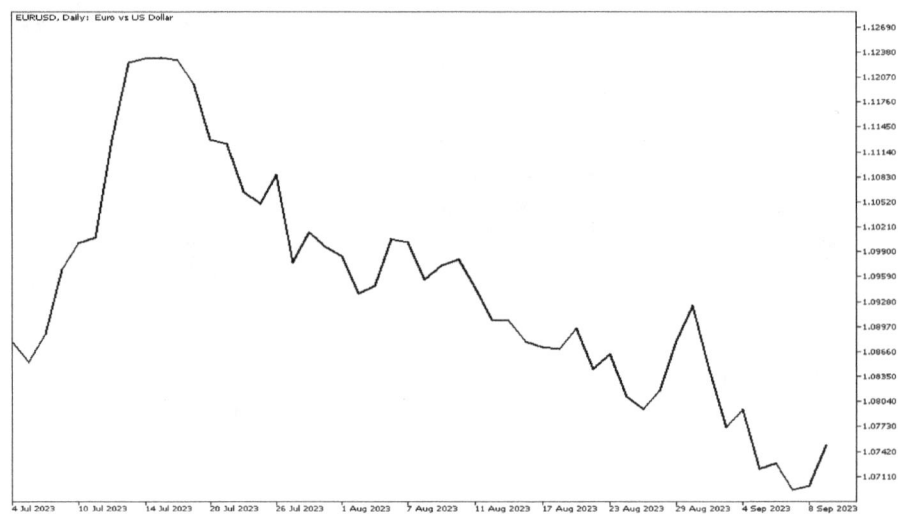

Bar Charts:

- **Description:** Bar charts display the opening, closing, high, and low prices for a currency pair over a specific period. Each bar represents a single period and consists of a vertical line and two horizontal lines.
- **Usage:** Bar charts provide more detailed information than line charts, allowing traders to analyze price ranges and intraday movements.

Candlestick Charts:

- **Description:** Candlestick charts are similar to bar charts but use 'candlesticks' to represent price data. Each candlestick shows the opening, closing, high, and low prices, with a body representing the difference between the opening and closing prices.
- **Usage:** Candlestick charts are popular among traders for their visual appeal and the ability to identify patterns and trends. They provide detailed insights into market sentiment and price action.

Time Frames

Minute Charts:

- **Description:** Minute charts represent price movements within a single minute. Common intervals include 1-minute, 5-minute, and 15-minute charts.
- **Usage:** Minute charts are used for short-term trading strategies and day trading. They help traders capture quick price movements and capitalize on short-term opportunities.

Hourly Charts:

- **Description:** Hourly charts display price movements within an hour. Common intervals include 1-hour, 4-hour, and 8-hour charts.
- **Usage:** Hourly charts are suitable for medium-term trading strategies. They help traders identify trends and patterns over a day or a few days.

Daily Charts:

- **Description:** Daily charts represent price movements within a single day.
- **Usage:** Daily charts are used for long-term trading strategies and position trading. They help traders identify major trends and long-term price movements.

Weekly Charts:

- **Description:** Weekly charts display price movements within a week.
- **Usage:** Weekly charts are suitable for very long-term trading strategies and investments. They provide a broad view of market trends and cycles.

3.2 Technical Indicators

Technical indicators are mathematical calculations based on historical price data. They help traders identify trends, momentum, volatility, and potential reversals.

Moving Averages:

- **Description:** Moving averages smooth out price data to identify the direction of the trend. There are two main types: Simple Moving Average (SMA) and Exponential Moving Average (EMA).
- **Usage:** Moving averages help traders identify trend direction and potential entry/exit points. They can also be used to identify support and resistance levels.

Relative Strength Index (RSI):

- **Description:** RSI is a momentum oscillator that measures the speed and change of price movements. It ranges from 0 to 100 and indicates overbought or oversold conditions.
- **Usage:** RSI values above 70 suggest overbought conditions, while values below 30 indicate oversold conditions. Traders use RSI to identify potential reversals and entry/exit points.

Bollinger Bands:

- **Description:** Bollinger Bands consist of a moving average and two standard deviation lines plotted above and below it. They measure market volatility.
- **Usage:** Bollinger Bands help traders identify overbought and oversold conditions, as well as potential breakouts. When prices move outside the bands, it may signal a reversal or continuation of the trend.

Fibonacci Retracement:

- **Description:** Fibonacci retracement levels are horizontal lines that indicate potential support and resistance levels based on the Fibonacci sequence.
- **Usage:** Traders use Fibonacci retracement levels to identify potential reversal points and entry/exit levels during a retracement within a larger trend.

3.3 Chart Patterns

Chart patterns are specific formations created by price movements on a chart. They help traders predict future price movements based on historical patterns.

Head and Shoulders:

- **Description:** The head and shoulders pattern is a reversal pattern consisting of three peaks: a higher peak (head) between two lower peaks (shoulders).
- **Usage:** This pattern indicates a potential reversal from an uptrend to a downtrend. Traders look for a break below the neckline (support level) to confirm the reversal.

Double Tops and Bottoms:

- **Description:** Double tops are bearish reversal patterns formed by two consecutive peaks at roughly the same price level. Double bottoms are bullish reversal patterns formed by two consecutive troughs at roughly the same price level.
- **Usage:** Double tops indicate a potential reversal from an uptrend to a downtrend, while double bottoms indicate a reversal from a downtrend to an uptrend. Traders look for a break of the neckline (support/resistance level) to confirm the reversal.

Triangles:

- **Description:** Triangles are continuation patterns formed by converging trendlines. There are three types: ascending, descending, and symmetrical triangles.
- **Usage:** Triangles indicate a period of consolidation before the price breaks out in the direction of the previous trend. Traders look for a break of the trendline to confirm the continuation.

Flags and Pennants:

- **Description:** Flags are small rectangular continuation patterns that form after a sharp price movement. Pennants are small symmetrical triangles that form after a sharp price movement.
- **Usage:** Flags and pennants indicate a brief consolidation period before the price continues in the direction of the previous trend. Traders look for a break of the pattern to confirm the continuation.

In summary, technical analysis in Forex involves using various chart types and time frames to visualize price movements, applying technical indicators to identify trends and potential reversals, and recognizing chart patterns to predict future price movements. Mastering these tools and techniques is essential for making informed trading decisions.

Chapter 4: Trading Strategies in Forex

4.1 Day Trading

Day trading involves making multiple trades within a single day, closing all positions before the market closes. This strategy relies on short-term price movements and requires constant monitoring of the market.

Scalping

Description:

- Scalping is a form of day trading where traders make dozens or hundreds of trades within a single day, aiming to profit from small price changes.

Characteristics:

- Trades are held for a few seconds to a few minutes.
- Requires high liquidity and tight spreads to be effective.
- Traders use high leverage to maximize returns on small price movements.

Techniques:

- **Order Flow Analysis:** Understanding the supply and demand dynamics by analyzing the order book.
- **Technical Indicators:** Using indicators like moving averages, Bollinger Bands, and RSI to identify entry and exit points.
- **Automated Trading:** Using algorithms to execute trades quickly and efficiently.

Intraday Strategies

Description:

- Intraday strategies involve opening and closing trades within the same day, focusing on exploiting short-term market movements.

Common Strategies:

- **Breakout Trading:** Identifying key levels of support and resistance and entering trades when the price breaks through these levels.
- **Momentum Trading:** Capitalizing on strong price movements in the direction of the trend, using indicators like RSI and MACD.
- **Reversal Trading:** Identifying potential reversal points using candlestick patterns, Fibonacci retracements, and divergence indicators.

4.2 Swing Trading

Swing trading involves holding positions for several days to weeks, aiming to profit from medium-term price movements.

Identifying Trends

Description:

- Identifying and trading in the direction of the prevailing trend.

Techniques:

- **Trend Lines:** Drawing trend lines to connect higher lows in an uptrend and lower highs in a downtrend.
- **Moving Averages:** Using moving averages to smooth out price data and identify trend direction.
- **Trend Indicators:** Using indicators like ADX (Average Directional Index) to measure the strength of a trend.

Using Support and Resistance Levels

Description:

- Identifying key levels where the price tends to reverse or consolidate.

Techniques:

- **Horizontal Levels:** Drawing horizontal lines at historical highs and lows to identify support and resistance levels.
- **Dynamic Levels:** Using moving averages and trend lines as dynamic support and resistance levels.
- **Pivot Points:** Calculating pivot points to identify potential reversal levels.

4.3 Position Trading

Position trading involves holding trades for months to years, focusing on long-term trends and fundamental analysis.

Long-Term Trends

Description:

- Identifying and trading based on long-term trends in the market.

Techniques:

- **Weekly and Monthly Charts:** Using higher time frames to identify long-term trends.
- **Trend Indicators:** Using indicators like MACD and long-term moving averages to confirm trend direction.

Fundamental Analysis Integration

Description:

- Combining technical analysis with fundamental analysis to make informed trading decisions.

Techniques:

- **Economic Indicators:** Monitoring key economic indicators like GDP, inflation, and interest rates.
- **Central Bank Policies:** Understanding central bank policies and their impact on currency values.
- **Geopolitical Events:** Keeping track of geopolitical events and their potential impact on the Forex market.

4.4 Risk Management

Effective risk management is crucial for long-term success in Forex trading. It involves setting stop-loss orders, proper position sizing, and diversification.

Setting Stop-Loss Orders

Description:

- A stop-loss order is an order placed to sell a security when it reaches a certain price, limiting potential losses.

Techniques:

- **Fixed Stop-Loss:** Setting a predetermined stop-loss level based on a fixed number of pips.
- **Trailing Stop-Loss:** Setting a stop-loss that trails the market price by a certain percentage or number of pips.
- **Volatility-Based Stop-Loss:** Adjusting stop-loss levels based on market volatility, using indicators like ATR (Average True Range).

Position Sizing

Description:

- Determining the appropriate amount of capital to allocate to each trade based on risk tolerance and account size.

Techniques:

- **Fixed Dollar Amount:** Allocating a fixed dollar amount to each trade.
- **Percentage of Account:** Risking a fixed percentage of the trading account on each trade.
- **Volatility-Based Position Sizing:** Adjusting position size based on market volatility, using indicators like ATR.

Diversification

Description:

- Spreading investments across different currency pairs and asset classes to reduce risk.

Techniques:

- **Currency Pair Diversification:** Trading multiple currency pairs to reduce exposure to any single currency.
- **Asset Class Diversification:** Investing in different asset classes, such as stocks, bonds, and commodities, to spread risk.
- **Geographic Diversification:** Trading currencies from different regions to mitigate regional economic risks.

Chapter 5: Forex Trading Platforms and Tools

5.1 Choosing a Forex Broker

Selecting the right Forex broker is crucial for successful trading. Key factors to consider include regulation, trading fees, and leverage requirements.

Regulation and Security

Description:

- Ensuring the broker is regulated by reputable financial authorities to ensure security and transparency.

Key Regulators:

- **NFA (National Futures Association):** United States
- **FCA (Financial Conduct Authority):** United Kingdom
- **ASIC (Australian Securities and Investments Commission):** Australia
- **CySEC (Cyprus Securities and Exchange Commission):** Cyprus

Trading Fees and Spreads

Description:

- Understanding the costs associated with trading, including spreads, commissions, and other fees.

Considerations:

- **Spreads:** The difference between the bid and ask prices. Lower spreads reduce trading costs.
- **Commissions:** Some brokers charge a commission per trade in addition to spreads.
- **Additional Fees:** Be aware of other fees, such as withdrawal fees, inactivity fees, and overnight financing charges.

Leverage and Margin Requirements

Description:

- Leverage allows traders to control a larger position with a smaller amount of capital. Margin is the collateral required to open a leveraged position.

Considerations:

- **Leverage Ratios:** Higher leverage increases potential profits but also increases risk.
- **Margin Requirements:** Understanding margin calls and how much capital is needed to maintain open positions.

5.2 Trading Platforms

Trading platforms are software applications that provide access to the Forex market. Key features to consider include ease of use, analytical tools, and execution speed.

MetaTrader 4 and 5

Description:

- MetaTrader 4 (MT4) and MetaTrader 5 (MT5) are popular trading platforms known for their user-friendly interface and advanced analytical tools.

Features:

- **Charting Tools:** Advanced charting capabilities with multiple time frames and technical indicators.
- **Automated Trading:** Support for Expert Advisors (EAs) to automate trading strategies.
- **Backtesting:** Ability to test trading strategies using historical data.

TradingView

Description:

- TradingView is a web-based platform offering advanced charting tools and social trading features.

Features:

- **Charting Tools:** High-quality charts with a wide range of technical indicators and drawing tools.
- **Social Trading:** Community features allowing traders to share ideas and strategies.
- **Accessibility:** Accessible from any device with an internet connection.

Broker-Specific Platforms

Description:

- Many brokers offer their proprietary trading platforms tailored to their services and features.

Features:

- **Customization:** Platforms may offer unique features and tools specific to the broker.
- **Integration:** Seamless integration with broker services, such as account management and customer support.
- **Ease of Use:** User-friendly interfaces designed for the broker's clientele.

5.3 Using Trading Tools

Trading tools provide additional information and analysis to help traders make informed decisions.

Economic Calendars

Description:

- Economic calendars provide schedules of key economic events and data releases that can impact the Forex market.

Features:

- **Event Alerts:** Notifications of upcoming economic events and data releases.
- **Impact Indicators:** Information on the potential impact of events on the market.
- **Historical Data:** Access to past economic data and its market impact.

News Feeds

Description:

- News feeds provide real-time updates on global financial news and events that can influence currency prices.

Features:

- **Real-Time Updates:** Instant access to breaking news and market-moving events.
- **Analysis:** Expert analysis and commentary on news events and their potential impact.
- **Customization:** Ability to filter news based on relevance to specific currencies or markets.

Analytical Tools

Description:

- Analytical tools offer advanced analysis of market data to help traders identify trends and potential trading opportunities.

Features:

- **Technical Indicators:** A wide range of indicators to analyze price movements and trends.
- **Chart Patterns:** Tools to identify and analyze chart patterns.
- **Backtesting:** Ability to test trading strategies using historical data to evaluate performance.

In summary, successful Forex trading involves selecting the right trading strategies, effectively managing risk, choosing a reliable broker, and using robust trading platforms and tools. Mastery of these aspects is essential for achieving long-term success in the Forex market.

Part 2: Understanding Cryptocurrency Trading

Chapter 6: The Basics of Cryptocurrency Trading

6.1 What are Cryptocurrencies?

Definition of Cryptocurrencies:

- Cryptocurrencies are digital or virtual currencies that use cryptography for security. Unlike traditional currencies issued by governments, cryptocurrencies operate on decentralized networks based on blockchain technology. This decentralized nature means that no single entity, such as a central bank, controls the supply or value of cryptocurrencies.

Brief History (Bitcoin and Altcoins):

- **Bitcoin (BTC):** Introduced in 2009 by an unknown individual or group using the pseudonym Satoshi Nakamoto, Bitcoin was the first cryptocurrency. It was designed to be a peer-to-peer electronic cash system that allows online payments to be sent directly from one party to another without going through a financial institution. Bitcoin's creation was a response to the 2008 financial crisis and aimed to offer an alternative to traditional banking systems.
- **Altcoins:** Following the success of Bitcoin, numerous alternative cryptocurrencies, known as altcoins, have been developed. These altcoins often aim to improve upon Bitcoin's technology or offer new features and use cases. Examples of popular altcoins include:
    - **Ethereum (ETH):** Introduced in 2015, Ethereum offers a decentralized platform for building and executing smart contracts and decentralized applications (dApps).
    - **Ripple (XRP):** Created to facilitate real-time, cross-border payment systems, Ripple aims to provide a frictionless experience for sending money globally.
    - **Litecoin (LTC):** Often referred to as the silver to Bitcoin's gold, Litecoin was created in 2011 and offers faster transaction confirmation times and a different hashing algorithm.

Blockchain Technology:

- Blockchain is the underlying technology that powers cryptocurrencies. It is a distributed ledger that records all transactions across a network of computers. Each block in the blockchain contains a list of transactions, and these blocks are linked together in chronological order to form a chain. The key features of blockchain technology include:
    - **Decentralization:** Blockchain operates on a decentralized network of computers (nodes) that collectively maintain the ledger. This eliminates the need for a central authority, reducing the risk of fraud and censorship.

- **Immutability:** Once a block is added to the blockchain, the information it contains cannot be altered. This ensures the integrity and transparency of the transaction history.
- **Security:** Cryptographic techniques secure the data on the blockchain, making it highly resistant to hacking and fraud. Each transaction is verified by network participants through a consensus mechanism (such as Proof of Work or Proof of Stake).

Understanding these fundamental aspects of cryptocurrencies is crucial for anyone looking to engage in cryptocurrency trading. The next sections will delve into how cryptocurrency trading works, the major cryptocurrencies in the market, and the analysis techniques used to evaluate them.

6.2 How Cryptocurrency Trading Works

Cryptocurrency Exchanges:

- Cryptocurrency exchanges are online platforms where users can buy, sell, and trade cryptocurrencies. These exchanges function similarly to traditional stock exchanges but specifically for digital assets. There are two main types of cryptocurrency exchanges:
    - **Centralized Exchanges (CEXs):** These are managed by a central authority or company. Examples include Binance, Coinbase, and Kraken. Centralized exchanges offer high liquidity, user-friendly interfaces, and various trading pairs but require users to trust the exchange with their funds.
    - **Decentralized Exchanges (DEXs):** These operate without a central authority, allowing peer-to-peer trading directly between users. Examples include Uniswap and Sushiswap. DEXs offer greater privacy and control over funds but may have lower liquidity and be more complex to use.

Trading Pairs (BTC/USD, ETH/BTC):

- **Trading pairs** refer to the two assets that are being traded against each other. The first currency in the pair is the base currency, and the second is the quote currency. The pair shows how much of the quote currency is needed to buy one unit of the base currency.
    - **BTC/USD:** This pair represents the price of Bitcoin in US Dollars. If BTC/USD is trading at $30,000, it means one Bitcoin is worth $30,000.
    - **ETH/BTC:** This pair represents the price of Ethereum in Bitcoin. If ETH/BTC is trading at 0.03, it means one Ethereum is worth 0.03 Bitcoin.

Market Orders and Limit Orders:

- **Market Orders:** These orders execute immediately at the current market price. They are used when the trader wants to buy or sell an asset quickly. Market orders prioritize speed

and guarantee execution but may result in less favorable prices, especially in volatile markets.
    - Example: If you place a market order to buy 1 BTC at the current price of $30,000, it will be executed immediately at the best available price.
- **Limit Orders:** These orders execute only at a specified price or better. They allow traders to set the maximum price they are willing to pay for a buy order or the minimum price they are willing to accept for a sell order. Limit orders provide more control over the execution price but do not guarantee execution if the market does not reach the specified price.
    - Example: If you place a limit order to buy 1 BTC at $28,000, the order will only execute if the price of Bitcoin drops to $28,000 or lower.

Liquidity and Volatility:

- **Liquidity:** Liquidity refers to the ease with which an asset can be bought or sold in the market without affecting its price. High liquidity indicates that there are many buyers and sellers in the market, allowing for quick and efficient transactions. Major cryptocurrencies like Bitcoin and Ethereum generally have high liquidity.
    - High liquidity benefits traders by reducing the risk of price slippage (the difference between the expected price of a trade and the actual price).
- **Volatility:** Volatility is the degree of variation in an asset's price over time. Cryptocurrencies are known for their high volatility, meaning their prices can experience significant fluctuations in short periods. While volatility presents opportunities for traders to profit from price swings, it also increases the risk of losses.
    - Example: The price of Bitcoin can move by several percentage points within a single day, providing opportunities for day traders but posing risks for long-term investors.

Understanding these fundamental aspects of how cryptocurrency trading works is crucial for navigating the market and making informed trading decisions. The next sections will cover major cryptocurrencies, fundamental analysis, and technical analysis techniques used in the cryptocurrency market.

6.3 Major Cryptocurrencies

Bitcoin (BTC):

- **Overview:** Bitcoin is the first and most well-known cryptocurrency, often referred to as digital gold. It was created by an unknown person or group using the pseudonym Satoshi Nakamoto and released as open-source software in 2009.
- **Technology:** Bitcoin operates on a decentralized peer-to-peer network, utilizing blockchain technology to record transactions. It employs a consensus mechanism known as Proof of Work (PoW), where miners validate transactions and secure the network by solving complex mathematical problems.

- **Use Case:** Bitcoin is primarily used as a store of value and a medium of exchange. Its limited supply of 21 million coins and decentralized nature make it an attractive hedge against inflation and a potential alternative to traditional fiat currencies.
- **Market Position:** As the first cryptocurrency, Bitcoin has the largest market capitalization and the most extensive adoption. It is widely accepted by merchants, integrated into financial systems, and considered the benchmark for other cryptocurrencies.

Ethereum (ETH):

- **Overview:** Ethereum is a decentralized platform that enables the creation and execution of smart contracts and decentralized applications (dApps). It was proposed by Vitalik Buterin in late 2013 and development began in early 2014, with the network going live in July 2015.
- **Technology:** Ethereum's blockchain is similar to Bitcoin's but with additional functionality to support smart contracts. It initially used the PoW consensus mechanism but is transitioning to Proof of Stake (PoS) with the Ethereum 2.0 upgrade to improve scalability and reduce energy consumption.
- **Use Case:** Ethereum's primary use case is as a platform for building and running dApps and smart contracts. These applications can automate processes, execute agreements without intermediaries, and create decentralized financial systems (DeFi).
- **Market Position:** Ethereum is the second-largest cryptocurrency by market capitalization and is considered the leading platform for smart contracts and dApps. Its versatility and developer community have made it a foundation for many other blockchain projects.

Ripple (XRP):

- **Overview:** Ripple is both a digital payment protocol and a cryptocurrency (XRP). It was created by Ripple Labs in 2012 to facilitate fast, low-cost international money transfers.
- **Technology:** Ripple's network, known as RippleNet, uses a consensus ledger and a unique consensus algorithm called the Ripple Protocol Consensus Algorithm (RPCA). Unlike Bitcoin and Ethereum, Ripple does not use mining, making transactions faster and more energy-efficient.
- **Use Case:** Ripple aims to provide a seamless experience for sending money globally by connecting banks, payment providers, and digital asset exchanges. XRP is used as a bridge currency to facilitate these transactions, providing liquidity and reducing costs.
- **Market Position:** Ripple has established partnerships with numerous financial institutions and is recognized for its potential to revolutionize cross-border payments. XRP is among the top cryptocurrencies by market capitalization.

Litecoin (LTC):

- **Overview:** Litecoin is a peer-to-peer cryptocurrency created by Charlie Lee in 2011 as a "lite" version of Bitcoin. It was designed to provide faster transaction confirmations and a more accessible mining process.

- **Technology:** Litecoin is based on Bitcoin's code but with some key differences. It uses the Scrypt hashing algorithm instead of SHA-256, making it easier for regular users to mine. Litecoin's block generation time is 2.5 minutes, compared to Bitcoin's 10 minutes.
- **Use Case:** Litecoin serves as a digital currency for everyday transactions. Its faster block times and lower transaction fees make it more suitable for smaller, everyday purchases compared to Bitcoin.
- **Market Position:** Litecoin is often referred to as the silver to Bitcoin's gold. It maintains a strong position in the market due to its longevity, active development community, and use as a testbed for new Bitcoin features.

These major cryptocurrencies each have unique characteristics, use cases, and positions within the market. Understanding their differences and roles is crucial for anyone looking to trade or invest in the cryptocurrency space. The next chapters will delve into the analysis techniques used to evaluate these assets, including fundamental and technical analysis.

Chapter 7: Fundamental Analysis in Cryptocurrency

7.1 Evaluating Cryptocurrencies

Fundamental analysis in cryptocurrency involves assessing the underlying factors that contribute to a cryptocurrency's value and potential for growth. Here are key aspects to consider:

Whitepapers:

- **Definition:** Whitepapers are detailed documents released by cryptocurrency projects that explain their technology, purpose, and vision. They outline the technical aspects, including the underlying blockchain technology, consensus mechanisms, tokenomics (token economics), and the problem the project aims to solve.
- **Importance:** Whitepapers provide essential insights into the project's goals, technical implementation, and potential challenges. They help investors and analysts understand the innovation and uniqueness of the cryptocurrency project.
- **Evaluation:** When evaluating a cryptocurrency, read its whitepaper thoroughly. Look for clear explanations of the technology, the problem it addresses, the roadmap for development, and the credentials of the team behind it. A well-written and technically sound whitepaper can indicate a strong and viable project.

Development Teams:

- **Role:** The development team plays a crucial role in the success of a cryptocurrency project. They are responsible for building, maintaining, and upgrading the blockchain network, smart contracts, and decentralized applications (dApps).
- **Evaluation:** Assess the experience, expertise, and track record of the development team. Look for team members with backgrounds in blockchain technology, cryptography,

software development, and relevant industries. Active and transparent communication from the team is also a positive indicator.
- **Community and Contributions:** Evaluate the level of community engagement and contributions to the project. Active participation in open-source development, GitHub repositories, and community forums can demonstrate the team's dedication and ability to deliver on promises.

Use Cases and Adoption:

- **Utility and Practical Applications:** Evaluate the real-world applications and utility of the cryptocurrency. Consider whether it solves a significant problem or improves upon existing solutions. Assess the potential demand for the cryptocurrency based on its use cases.
- **Adoption and Partnerships:** Monitor the adoption rate of the cryptocurrency and partnerships with established institutions, businesses, or governments. Partnerships can enhance credibility, expand use cases, and drive adoption.
- **Network Effect:** A strong network effect, where more users and businesses adopt the cryptocurrency, can increase its value and utility. Look for indications of growing usage and acceptance in various sectors.

Fundamental analysis in cryptocurrency involves synthesizing information from whitepapers, evaluating the development team's capabilities, and assessing the cryptocurrency's use cases and adoption. These factors provide insights into the long-term viability and potential growth of a cryptocurrency project. Understanding these fundamentals is essential for making informed investment decisions in the dynamic and evolving cryptocurrency market.

7.2 Market Sentiment

Understanding market sentiment is crucial in cryptocurrency trading and investment. It refers to the overall attitude or feeling of investors and traders towards a particular cryptocurrency or the market as a whole. Here are key aspects of market sentiment:

Media Influence:

- **Impact:** Media outlets, including news websites, TV channels, and social media platforms, can significantly influence cryptocurrency prices and market sentiment. Positive or negative news coverage, regulatory announcements, technological advancements, or security breaches can lead to rapid price movements.
- **Analysis:** Monitor reputable sources for accurate and timely information. Be cautious of sensationalized news and verify information from multiple sources before making trading decisions. Understanding how media narratives can shape market sentiment helps traders anticipate market reactions.

Social Media and Forums:

- **Role:** Social media platforms like Twitter, Reddit, and Telegram, as well as cryptocurrency-specific forums and communities, play a vital role in shaping market sentiment. Discussions, opinions, and rumors spread quickly and can impact trading volumes and prices.
- **Sentiment Analysis:** Tools and techniques, such as sentiment analysis algorithms, track and analyze social media posts and forum discussions to gauge public sentiment. Positive sentiment may indicate bullish trends, while negative sentiment could signal potential market downturns.
- **Caution:** Social media sentiment can be volatile and influenced by emotions. Consider the credibility of sources, the size of the community, and the level of engagement before basing trading decisions solely on social media sentiment.

Market Psychology:

- **Emotions and Behavior:** Market psychology refers to the collective emotions, biases, and behaviors of market participants. Greed, fear, optimism, and pessimism influence buying and selling decisions, impacting market trends and price movements.
- **Patterns:** Psychological phenomena, such as FOMO (Fear of Missing Out) and FUD (Fear, Uncertainty, Doubt), often drive short-term volatility in cryptocurrency markets. Understanding these patterns helps traders anticipate market reactions and make informed decisions.
- **Contrarian Indicators:** Contrarian traders may use market psychology to identify opportunities. Extreme sentiment levels (e.g., widespread fear or excessive optimism) may signal potential market reversals or buying opportunities.

Incorporating an understanding of market sentiment, media influence, social media dynamics, and market psychology into your cryptocurrency analysis can provide valuable insights into market trends and potential price movements. It complements technical and fundamental analysis, helping traders navigate the volatile and rapidly evolving cryptocurrency markets effectively.

7.3 Regulatory Environment

The regulatory environment plays a critical role in shaping the cryptocurrency market's landscape, affecting everything from market stability to investor confidence. Here are key aspects to consider:

Government Regulations:

- **Varied Approaches:** Governments worldwide have adopted varying approaches to regulate cryptocurrencies, ranging from outright bans to embracing and integrating them into existing financial systems.

- **Objectives:** Regulatory objectives typically include consumer protection, preventing financial crimes (such as money laundering and terrorism financing), ensuring market integrity, and promoting innovation while managing risks.
- **Impact:** Regulatory actions, such as introducing licensing requirements for exchanges, imposing taxes on cryptocurrency transactions, or restricting ICOs (Initial Coin Offerings), can impact market liquidity, trading volumes, and investor sentiment.

Legal Status of Cryptocurrencies:

- **Undefined or Uncertain:** The legal status of cryptocurrencies varies widely across jurisdictions. Some countries classify cryptocurrencies as legal tender, digital assets, commodities, or securities, while others have not yet defined their legal status.
- **Legal Clarity:** Clarity in regulatory frameworks provides certainty to market participants and fosters mainstream adoption. Conversely, ambiguity or conflicting regulations can create uncertainty and deter institutional investors and businesses from entering the market.
- **Global Coordination:** As cryptocurrencies are global in nature, regulatory developments in one jurisdiction can have ripple effects globally. International cooperation and standards can help address regulatory arbitrage and promote consistent practices.

Impact on the Market:

- **Market Reaction:** Regulatory announcements and developments often trigger significant market reactions, causing price volatility and affecting trading volumes. Positive regulatory news, such as regulatory clarity or supportive frameworks, can boost market confidence and lead to price rallies.
- **Long-Term Implications:** Stable and supportive regulatory environments can encourage institutional investment and adoption, contributing to market maturation and growth. Conversely, stringent regulations or bans may hinder innovation and limit market expansion.

Navigating Regulatory Risks:

- **Due Diligence:** Stay informed about regulatory developments and understand the legal landscape in jurisdictions relevant to your investments or trading activities.
- **Adaptation:** Cryptocurrency projects and exchanges must comply with evolving regulatory requirements to mitigate risks and build trust with regulators and users.
- **Industry Advocacy:** Industry associations and stakeholders advocate for clear and balanced regulations that foster innovation while addressing regulatory concerns.

Understanding the regulatory environment is essential for assessing risks and opportunities in the cryptocurrency market. It informs investment decisions, risk management strategies, and long-term planning, ensuring compliance and navigating legal complexities effectively.

Chapter 8: Technical Analysis in Cryptocurrency

8.1 Chart Types and Time Frames

Technical analysis in cryptocurrency involves studying historical price and volume data to forecast future price movements. Understanding chart types and time frames is fundamental to this analysis:

Similarities with Forex Charting:

- **Common Chart Types:** Cryptocurrency trading shares several chart types with forex trading, including:
    - **Line Charts:** Show the closing prices over a period, useful for identifying trends.
    - **Bar Charts:** Display high, low, open, and close prices for each period, providing more detailed information than line charts.
    - **Candlestick Charts:** Offer the same data as bar charts but in a visual format that highlights price movements. Candlestick patterns are widely used in technical analysis for trend recognition and reversal signals.
- **Technical Indicators:** Many technical indicators used in forex trading, such as moving averages (MA), Relative Strength Index (RSI), and Fibonacci retracement levels, are also applicable to cryptocurrency charts. These tools help traders analyze price trends, momentum, and potential support/resistance levels.

Unique Aspects of Crypto Charts:

- **Market Hours:** Unlike forex markets, which operate 24/5, cryptocurrency markets are open 24/7. This continuous trading creates unique patterns and price movements influenced by global news and events.
- **Volatility:** Cryptocurrencies are known for their high volatility, which can lead to rapid price fluctuations and short-term trading opportunities. Technical analysis helps traders navigate these volatile markets by identifying entry and exit points based on price patterns and indicators.
- **Liquidity Challenges:** Some cryptocurrencies may have lower liquidity compared to major forex pairs, impacting price stability and execution speed. Traders should consider liquidity when analyzing charts and executing trades.
- **Sentiment Analysis:** social media and online forums play a significant role in shaping cryptocurrency prices. Technical analysts often incorporate sentiment analysis alongside traditional charting techniques to gauge market sentiment and anticipate price movements.

Understanding these similarities and unique aspects of cryptocurrency charts is essential for applying effective technical analysis. Traders should adapt their strategies based on market conditions, volatility, and the specific characteristics of the cryptocurrencies they are trading. Technical analysis serves as a valuable tool for making informed trading decisions in the dynamic and evolving cryptocurrency market.

Chapter 8: Technical Analysis in Cryptocurrency

8.2 Technical Indicators

Technical indicators are tools used by traders and analysts to interpret historical price data and forecast future price movements in cryptocurrency markets. Here are some commonly used technical indicators:

Moving Averages:

- **Definition:** Moving averages (MA) smooth out price data by creating a constantly updated average price. They help traders identify trends and potential reversals by filtering out noise from random price fluctuations.
- **Types:**
  - **Simple Moving Average (SMA):** Calculates the average price over a specified number of periods equally.
  - **Exponential Moving Average (EMA):** Gives more weight to recent prices, making it more responsive to recent price changes.
- **Use:** Traders use moving averages to determine trend direction (upward or downward), identify support and resistance levels, and generate buy/sell signals based on crossovers and price interactions with moving averages.

RSI (Relative Strength Index):

- **Definition:** RSI is a momentum oscillator that measures the speed and change of price movements. It oscillates between 0 and 100 and is typically used to identify overbought or oversold conditions in a market.
- **Interpretation:**
  - RSI values above 70 indicate overbought conditions, suggesting a potential price reversal or correction.
  - RSI values below 30 indicate oversold conditions, suggesting a potential buying opportunity or price bounce.
- **Use:** Traders use RSI to confirm trends, spot divergence between price and momentum, and anticipate potential reversals or continuation patterns.

MACD (Moving Average Convergence Divergence):

- **Definition:** MACD is a trend-following momentum indicator that shows the relationship between two moving averages of a security's price.
- **Components:**
  - **MACD Line:** The difference between a short-term EMA (typically 12 periods) and a long-term EMA (typically 26 periods).
  - **Signal Line:** A 9-period EMA of the MACD line.
  - **Histogram:** Shows the difference between the MACD line and the signal line.

- **Use:** Traders use MACD to identify changes in trend direction, momentum shifts, and potential buy/sell signals based on crossovers and divergence between the MACD line and the signal line.

Volume Analysis:

- **Definition:** Volume measures the number of shares or contracts traded in a particular security or market over a specified period. In cryptocurrency trading, volume represents the amount of a cryptocurrency traded within a certain timeframe.
- **Use:**
  - High trading volume confirms the strength of a price movement, indicating widespread interest and participation.
  - Low trading volume may signal indecision or lack of market conviction, potentially foreshadowing trend reversals or consolidations.
- **Interpretation:** Traders analyze volume alongside price movements and technical indicators to validate trends, identify potential breakouts or reversals, and gauge market sentiment.

8.3 Chart Patterns

Chart patterns in cryptocurrency trading are visual representations of price movements over time, providing insights into potential future price movements. They can be categorized into patterns similar to those found in forex trading and unique patterns specific to cryptocurrencies:

Similarities with Forex Patterns:

- **Head and Shoulders:** A reversal pattern that indicates a potential trend reversal from bullish to bearish or vice versa.
- **Double Tops and Bottoms:** Patterns that signal potential reversal points, with two consecutive peaks (tops) or troughs (bottoms) indicating resistance or support levels.
- **Triangles:** Continuation patterns that show a period of consolidation before the price breaks out in the direction of the prevailing trend.
- **Flags and Pennants:** Short-term continuation patterns that occur after a strong price movement, indicating a brief consolidation before the trend resumes.

Unique Crypto Patterns:

- **Pump and Dump:** This pattern involves a sudden and significant increase (pump) in price followed by a rapid decline (dump) due to coordinated buying and selling, often associated with low-cap or less liquid cryptocurrencies.
- **Whales:** Price manipulation patterns caused by large holders (whales) of a cryptocurrency influencing market movements through significant buy or sell orders.
- **Altcoin Season:** Periods where altcoins (alternative cryptocurrencies other than Bitcoin) experience significant price increases relative to Bitcoin, often driven by shifts in market sentiment and investor interest.

Understanding these chart patterns helps traders identify potential entry and exit points, confirm trend directions, and manage risk effectively in cryptocurrency markets. Technical analysis, when combined with fundamental analysis and market sentiment, forms a comprehensive approach to trading cryptocurrencies.

Chapter 9: Trading Strategies in Cryptocurrency

9.1 Day Trading

Day trading in cryptocurrency involves executing multiple trades within a single trading day to profit from short-term price fluctuations. Here are two common day trading strategies:

Scalping in Crypto:

- **Objective:** Scalping aims to profit from small price changes by entering and exiting positions quickly, often within seconds to minutes.
- **Techniques:** Traders look for opportunities in high liquidity cryptocurrencies with tight bid-ask spreads. They may use technical indicators like moving averages, RSI, or MACD on short timeframes (e.g., 1-minute or 5-minute charts) to identify entry and exit points.
- **Risk Management:** Scalpers focus on high win rates with small profit margins per trade. Strict risk management, including setting tight stop-loss orders and avoiding emotional trading, is crucial due to the fast-paced nature of scalping.

Intraday Strategies:

- **Objective:** Intraday trading involves holding positions for a few hours to exploit price movements within the trading day.
- **Approaches:** Traders may use technical analysis tools such as chart patterns, support and resistance levels, and volume analysis to identify intraday trends and price reversals.
- **Execution:** Entry and exit points are based on technical signals and market conditions. Traders may also incorporate news catalysts and market sentiment into their intraday strategies.
- **Risk Management:** Intraday traders manage risk by setting stop-loss orders, diversifying their trades across multiple cryptocurrencies, and avoiding overnight exposure to market volatility.

9.2 Swing Trading

Swing trading in cryptocurrency focuses on capturing medium-term price movements over several days to weeks. It involves identifying and trading within established trends using support and resistance levels:

Identifying Trends in Crypto:

- **Objective:** Swing traders aim to profit from price swings within broader trends, whether bullish or bearish.

- **Analysis:** Technical analysis tools, such as moving averages (e.g., 50-day and 200-day SMAs), trendlines, and Fibonacci retracement levels, help identify and confirm trends.
- **Entry and Exit:** Traders enter positions after confirming a trend reversal or continuation pattern. They often wait for price retracements to key support levels in uptrends or resistance levels in downtrends before entering trades.
- **Risk Management:** Swing traders use wider stop-loss orders compared to day traders to accommodate market volatility. They may also scale positions based on the strength of the trend and adjust stop-loss levels as the trade progresses.

Using Support and Resistance Levels:

- **Definition:** Support levels indicate price levels where buying interest is strong enough to prevent further price declines. Resistance levels denote price levels where selling pressure prevents further price increases.
- **Application:** Swing traders use support and resistance levels to plan entry and exit points. They may buy near support levels during uptrends or sell near resistance levels during downtrends.
- **Confirmation:** Breakouts above resistance or below support levels can signal potential trend reversals or continuations, providing opportunities for swing traders to enter trades with momentum.

By employing these day trading and swing trading strategies, cryptocurrency traders can capitalize on short-term and medium-term price movements while managing risk through effective technical analysis and risk management techniques. Understanding market dynamics, liquidity considerations, and market sentiment is essential for successful implementation of these strategies in the dynamic cryptocurrency market.

9.3 Long-term Investing (HODLing)

Long-term investing in cryptocurrency, often referred to as "HODLing," involves buying and holding digital assets for extended periods with the expectation of significant price appreciation. Here's how to approach long-term investing in cryptocurrencies:

Buy and Hold Strategy:

- **Objective:** The primary goal of the buy and hold strategy is to accumulate cryptocurrencies that are expected to increase in value over time due to adoption, technological advancements, or market demand.
- **Selection Criteria:** Investors focus on identifying cryptocurrencies with strong fundamentals, including:
  - **Technology and Use Case:** Evaluate the project's underlying technology, blockchain scalability, security features, and its practical applications.
  - **Development Team:** Assess the credentials, experience, and transparency of the development team. Strong teams often contribute to project credibility and long-term success.

- **Community and Adoption:** Consider the size and engagement of the community supporting the cryptocurrency. High levels of adoption by users, developers, and businesses can indicate future growth potential.
- **Market Position:** Analyze the cryptocurrency's market position, competitive advantages, and potential for disruption within its industry or niche.

Strategy Execution:

- **Patience:** Long-term investors adopt a patient approach, holding through market fluctuations and short-term price volatility.
- **Diversification:** Spread investments across multiple cryptocurrencies to mitigate risk and capture opportunities across different sectors or use cases.
- **Portfolio Management:** Regularly review and rebalance your portfolio based on changes in market conditions, project developments, and new investment opportunities.

Identifying Strong Projects:

- **Research:** Conduct thorough research using reputable sources, whitepapers, project roadmaps, and community feedback to evaluate potential investments.
- **Fundamental Analysis:** Focus on fundamental factors such as the project's technology, team, community support, use cases, and competitive landscape.
- **Long-Term Potential:** Look for cryptocurrencies with robust long-term growth prospects, sustainable development strategies, and a clear vision for scalability and adoption.

Risk Management:

- **Risk Assessment:** Assess and manage risks associated with each investment, including regulatory changes, technological risks, market volatility, and macroeconomic factors.
- **Exit Strategy:** Define clear exit criteria based on your investment goals, such as target price levels, timeframes, or changes in project fundamentals.

Long-term investing in cryptocurrencies requires a disciplined approach, thorough research, and a long-term perspective on market trends and technology advancements. By identifying strong projects and executing a buy and hold strategy effectively, investors can potentially benefit from the growth and maturation of the cryptocurrency ecosystem over time.

9.4 Risk Management

Effective risk management is crucial in cryptocurrency trading and investing to protect capital and optimize returns. Here are key risk management strategies:

Setting Stop-Loss Orders:

- **Definition:** A stop-loss order is a risk management tool that automatically sells a cryptocurrency position when its price reaches a specified level, limiting potential losses.

- **Purpose:** Protects traders and investors from significant downside risk by exiting positions before losses exceed predetermined thresholds.
- **Types:**
  - **Fixed Percentage:** Sets the stop-loss order at a percentage below the entry price (e.g., 5% or 10%).
  - **Technical Levels:** Places stop-loss orders based on support levels, moving averages, or other technical indicators to align with market dynamics.
- **Implementation:** Adjust stop-loss levels based on market conditions, volatility, and individual risk tolerance. Regularly review and update stop-loss orders to reflect changing price movements and market sentiment.

Position Sizing:

- **Definition:** Position sizing determines the amount of capital allocated to each trade or investment based on risk tolerance and portfolio objectives.
- **Strategies:**
  - **Fixed Dollar Amount:** Allocates a fixed amount or percentage of total capital to each trade, ensuring consistent risk exposure regardless of trade size.
  - **Risk-based:** Calculates position size based on the distance between entry price and stop-loss level, maintaining a predetermined risk-to-reward ratio (e.g., risking 2% of capital per trade).
- **Diversification:** Spreads capital across multiple cryptocurrencies or trades to reduce portfolio risk and exposure to individual asset volatility.

Diversification in Crypto:

- **Benefits:** Diversification spreads risk across different cryptocurrencies, sectors, and investment strategies, reducing the impact of adverse price movements on overall portfolio performance.
- **Approach:**
  - **Asset Classes:** Allocate capital across major cryptocurrencies, stablecoins, and tokens with varying risk profiles and market correlations.
  - **Sector Diversification:** Invest in cryptocurrencies from different sectors (e.g., DeFi, NFTs, privacy coins) to mitigate sector-specific risks and capitalize on diverse growth opportunities.
  - **Geographic Exposure:** Consider exposure to cryptocurrencies from different geographic regions to manage regulatory risks and market-specific factors.
- **Monitoring:** Regularly monitor portfolio performance and rebalance holdings based on changing market conditions, new investment opportunities, and risk management goals.

Effective risk management in cryptocurrency trading involves a balanced approach to setting stop-loss orders, determining position sizes, and implementing diversification strategies. By proactively managing risk, traders and investors can protect capital, optimize returns, and navigate the dynamic and volatile cryptocurrency market with greater confidence.

Chapter 10: Cryptocurrency Trading Platforms and Tools

10.1 Choosing a Crypto Exchange

Selecting the right cryptocurrency exchange is essential for trading and investing safely and efficiently. Consider the following factors when choosing a crypto exchange:

Security and Regulation:

- **Security Measures:** Choose exchanges that prioritize security protocols such as two-factor authentication (2FA), cold storage for the majority of funds, and regular security audits.
- **Regulatory Compliance:** Opt for exchanges that adhere to regulatory requirements in their operating jurisdictions. Look for exchanges registered with financial authorities or compliant with relevant laws to mitigate regulatory risks.

Trading Fees and Spreads:

- **Fee Structure:** Evaluate trading fees, including maker and taker fees, withdrawal fees, and deposit fees. Lower fees can significantly impact trading profitability, especially for high-frequency traders.
- **Spreads:** Consider the difference between the buying (ask) and selling (bid) prices (spread). Lower spreads indicate better liquidity and tighter market conditions.

Supported Cryptocurrencies:

- **Variety:** Assess the range of cryptocurrencies supported by the exchange. Choose exchanges that offer a diverse selection of cryptocurrencies to trade, including major coins (e.g., Bitcoin, Ethereum) and altcoins across different sectors.
- **Listing Policy:** Understand the exchange's listing criteria and policies for adding new cryptocurrencies. Exchanges with transparent listing processes may offer opportunities to trade emerging digital assets.

Additional Considerations:

- **User Experience:** Evaluate the exchange's trading interface, mobile app functionality, and customer support responsiveness.
- **Liquidity:** Higher liquidity facilitates faster order execution and reduces the risk of slippage, particularly during volatile market conditions.
- **Geographical Restrictions:** Check if the exchange operates in your geographical region and supports fiat currency deposits and withdrawals if needed.

Research and Due Diligence:

- **Reviews and Feedback:** Research user reviews, industry reports, and feedback from other traders to gauge the exchange's reputation, reliability, and customer service.

- **Security Incidents:** Investigate any history of security breaches or operational issues reported by the exchange to assess its risk profile.

Choosing a reputable and reliable cryptocurrency exchange is critical to ensuring a secure and seamless trading experience. By prioritizing security, understanding fee structures, and assessing the variety of supported cryptocurrencies, traders can select an exchange that aligns with their trading goals and risk tolerance.

10.2 Trading Platforms

Cryptocurrency trading platforms play a pivotal role in facilitating trades and managing investments in digital assets. Here's an overview of three prominent platforms:

Binance

Overview:

- **Founded:** Binance was founded in 2017 by Changpeng Zhao and has quickly grown to become one of the largest cryptocurrency exchanges globally.
- **Features:** Binance offers a comprehensive range of trading services, including spot trading, futures trading, margin trading, staking, and a launchpad for token sales.
- **Supported Cryptocurrencies:** Binance supports a vast array of cryptocurrencies, including major coins like Bitcoin (BTC), Ethereum (ETH), and a wide selection of altcoins.
- **Security:** Binance employs robust security measures, including two-factor authentication (2FA), cold wallet storage for the majority of funds, and regular security audits.
- **User Experience:** Binance provides a user-friendly interface suitable for both novice and experienced traders, along with advanced charting tools and a mobile app for trading on the go.
- **Regulatory Compliance:** Binance operates globally and complies with local regulations in various jurisdictions, offering different versions of the exchange tailored to specific regions.

Coinbase

Overview:

- **Founded:** Coinbase is one of the oldest cryptocurrency exchanges, founded in 2012 by Brian Armstrong and Fred Ehrsam.
- **Features:** Coinbase primarily focuses on providing a user-friendly platform for buying, selling, and storing cryptocurrencies. It offers services for retail investors, institutions (Coinbase Pro), and developers (Coinbase Commerce).
- **Supported Cryptocurrencies:** Initially focused on major cryptocurrencies like Bitcoin and Ethereum, Coinbase has expanded to support a wide range of digital assets, including stablecoins and DeFi tokens.

- **Security:** Coinbase prioritizes security with measures such as offline cold storage, insurance coverage for digital assets, and regulatory compliance in multiple jurisdictions.
- **User Experience:** Known for its intuitive interface and educational resources, Coinbase is popular among beginners. Coinbase Pro offers advanced trading features, including charts, order books, and trading APIs.
- **Regulatory Compliance:** Coinbase adheres to regulatory standards in the United States and other countries where it operates, ensuring compliance with AML/KYC regulations.

Kraken

Overview:

- **Founded:** Kraken was founded in 2011 by Jesse Powell and is one of the oldest cryptocurrency exchanges still in operation.
- **Features:** Kraken offers a variety of trading options, including spot trading, futures trading, margin trading, and staking services. It also supports over 50 cryptocurrencies and provides access to trading pairs with fiat currencies.
- **Security:** Kraken emphasizes security, employing features such as cold storage for most funds, 2FA, and regular security audits by third-party firms.
- **User Experience:** Kraken provides a robust trading platform with advanced charting tools, customizable interfaces, and mobile apps for trading on iOS and Android devices.
- **Regulatory Compliance:** Kraken is known for its strong regulatory compliance framework, operating with licenses in various jurisdictions and adhering to legal and regulatory requirements globally.

Choosing the Right Platform

When selecting a cryptocurrency trading platform like Binance, Coinbase, or Kraken, consider factors such as security, supported cryptocurrencies, trading fees, user experience, and regulatory compliance. Each platform offers unique features tailored to different types of traders, from beginners to advanced users and institutional investors. Conduct thorough research, assess your trading needs and preferences, and choose a platform that aligns with your goals for trading and investing in cryptocurrencies.

10.3 Using Trading Tools

Trading tools are essential for cryptocurrency traders and investors to stay informed, manage portfolios effectively, and make data-driven decisions. Here's an overview of key trading tools:

Crypto News Aggregators

Purpose:

- **Information Source:** Crypto news aggregators compile news articles, updates, and insights from various sources, providing traders with real-time information on market trends, regulatory developments, and technological advancements.

- **Market Sentiment:** Track sentiment analysis based on news sentiment scores and community reactions to news events, influencing market movements.
- **Examples:** CoinDesk, CoinTelegraph, CryptoPanic, and NewsNowCrypto are popular crypto news aggregators.

Portfolio Trackers

Purpose:

- **Performance Monitoring:** Portfolio trackers enable traders to monitor the performance of their cryptocurrency investments in real-time, including profit and loss calculations, asset allocation, and historical performance analysis.
- **Diversification:** Track portfolio diversification across different cryptocurrencies, sectors, and asset classes to manage risk and optimize investment strategies.
- **Examples:** Blockfolio, Delta, CoinStats, and CoinTracking are widely used portfolio tracking apps with features like price alerts, transaction history, and tax reporting tools.

Analytical Tools

Purpose:

- **Technical Analysis:** Analytical tools provide charts, technical indicators, and trading signals to analyze price trends, identify patterns, and make informed trading decisions.
- **Market Data:** Access historical and real-time market data, including trading volumes, order book depth, and price movements across multiple cryptocurrency exchanges.
- **Examples:** TradingView, CryptoCompare, CoinGecko, and CoinMarketCap offer comprehensive analytical tools, charting capabilities, and market data insights for cryptocurrency traders.

Choosing and Using Trading Tools

- **Integration:** Integrate multiple trading tools to complement each other and enhance decision-making capabilities, combining news aggregation with technical analysis and portfolio tracking.
- **Customization:** Customize alerts, notifications, and dashboard layouts based on personal preferences and trading strategies.
- **Education:** Stay informed about new features and updates in trading tools, and continuously improve skills in using them effectively for cryptocurrency trading and investment.

By leveraging crypto news aggregators, portfolio trackers, and analytical tools, traders can stay ahead of market trends, manage their investments efficiently, and execute well-informed trading strategies in the dynamic cryptocurrency market. Each tool plays a crucial role in providing insights, monitoring performance, and maximizing opportunities for traders and investors alike.

Part 3: Advanced Topics in Forex and Cryptocurrency Trading

Chapter 11: Algorithmic Trading

Algorithmic trading, also known as algo trading or automated trading, revolutionizes trading by using computer algorithms to execute trades automatically based on predefined criteria. Here's an introduction to algorithmic trading:

11.1 Introduction to Algorithmic Trading

Definition and Benefits:

- **Definition:** Algorithmic trading refers to the use of algorithms or computer programs to automatically execute trading strategies in financial markets, including Forex and cryptocurrencies.
- **Benefits:**
    - **Speed:** Algorithms execute trades at speeds far exceeding human capabilities, leveraging high-frequency trading (HFT) techniques to capitalize on fleeting market opportunities.
    - **Accuracy:** Eliminates emotional biases and human errors, ensuring trades are executed based on predefined rules and criteria.
    - **Backtesting and Optimization:** Algorithms can be backtested using historical data to assess performance and optimize trading strategies before deployment.
    - **Diversification:** Allows for simultaneous execution of multiple strategies or trades across different assets or markets, enhancing portfolio diversification.

Types of Algorithms:

- **Execution Algorithms:** Focus on optimizing trade execution to achieve the best possible price with minimal market impact, including:
    - **TWAP (Time-Weighted Average Price):** Executes trades evenly over a specified time period to minimize impact on market prices.
    - **VWAP (Volume-Weighted Average Price):** Executes trades based on trading volume to achieve a benchmark price.
    - **Implementation Shortfall:** Balances trade-offs between price and execution speed to minimize costs.
- **Quantitative Strategies:** Utilize mathematical models and statistical analysis to identify trading opportunities, including:
    - **Mean Reversion:** Capitalizes on price reversals from historical averages.
    - **Trend Following:** Trades based on directional trends in asset prices.
    - **Arbitrage:** Exploits price differentials between markets or assets to generate profits with minimal risk.
- **High-Frequency Trading (HFT):** Executes large numbers of orders at extremely high speeds, often leveraging co-location and direct market access (DMA) to gain millisecond advantages in trading.

Algorithmic trading has transformed financial markets by enhancing efficiency, liquidity, and access for traders and investors. Understanding different types of algorithms and their applications is crucial for leveraging algorithmic trading effectively in both Forex and cryptocurrency markets.

11.2 Developing Trading Algorithms

Developing trading algorithms involves programming strategies in languages like Python or C++, and then rigorously testing and refining them through backtesting and optimization processes. Here's a detailed exploration of each component:

Programming Languages:

1. **Python:**
    - **Advantages:** Python is widely preferred for algorithmic trading due to its simplicity, readability, and extensive libraries for data analysis, machine learning, and integration with trading APIs.
    - **Libraries:** Utilize libraries like NumPy (for numerical computations), pandas (for data manipulation), scikit-learn (for machine learning), and libraries specific to financial data analysis (e.g., QuantLib, TA-Lib).
    - **API Integration:** Python interfaces well with trading platforms and APIs offered by brokers and exchanges, facilitating seamless trade execution and data retrieval.
2. **C++:**
    - **Advantages:** C++ is known for its speed, efficiency, and low-level control, making it suitable for high-frequency trading (HFT) algorithms and complex trading systems.
    - **Performance:** Offers superior performance in terms of execution speed and memory management, critical for handling large volumes of data and high-frequency trading strategies.
    - **Integration:** Often used in developing low-latency systems where microseconds matter, such as in HFT firms and institutional trading desks.

Backtesting and Optimization:

1. **Backtesting:**
    - **Purpose:** Backtesting involves testing a trading strategy using historical market data to evaluate its performance and profitability.
    - **Process:**
        - **Data Selection:** Choose relevant historical data (e.g., price, volume, order book data) for backtesting.
        - **Strategy Implementation:** Code the trading strategy in Python or C++, incorporating data preprocessing, signal generation, risk management rules, and trade execution logic.
        - **Performance Evaluation:** Measure strategy performance using metrics like profit and loss (P&L), Sharpe ratio, maximum drawdown, and win-loss ratio.

- **Simulation:** Simulate trading decisions based on historical data to assess strategy effectiveness, accounting for transaction costs, slippage, and market impact.

2. **Optimization:**
    - **Parameter Tuning:** Adjust strategy parameters (e.g., entry/exit thresholds, position sizing rules) to optimize performance metrics and enhance profitability.
    - **Iterative Testing:** Conduct iterative testing with different parameter sets to identify optimal configurations that yield consistent returns across various market conditions.
    - **Risk Management:** Integrate risk management techniques, such as stop-loss orders, position sizing algorithms, and portfolio diversification rules, into the optimization process to mitigate risks.

Best Practices:

- **Data Quality:** Use clean, accurate historical data and consider realistic market conditions for robust backtesting results.
- **Robustness Testing:** Test algorithms under different market scenarios, volatility levels, and economic environments to assess resilience and adaptability.
- **Documentation:** Maintain thorough documentation of trading algorithms, including code, strategy rationale, parameter settings, and performance metrics.
- **Continuous Improvement:** Regularly review and refine algorithms based on performance feedback from backtesting and live trading results, incorporating market insights and new data.

Developing effective trading algorithms requires proficiency in programming languages like Python or C++, combined with rigorous backtesting and optimization processes. By leveraging these tools and practices, traders can enhance decision-making capabilities, automate trading strategies, and potentially achieve consistent profitability in dynamic financial markets.

11.3 Implementing and Managing Algorithms

Implementing and managing trading algorithms involves selecting a suitable platform and establishing processes for monitoring and adjusting algorithms to ensure optimal performance. Here's a comprehensive guide:

Choosing a Platform:

1. **Algorithmic Trading Platforms:**
    - **Cloud-Based Platforms:** Platforms like AWS (Amazon Web Services), Google Cloud Platform, or Microsoft Azure offer cloud infrastructure for deploying and scaling trading algorithms.
    - **Broker-Specific Platforms:** Some brokers provide proprietary algorithmic trading platforms with integrated tools for strategy development, backtesting, and live trading.

- **Open-Source Platforms:** Utilize open-source platforms like QuantConnect, Quantopian, or Backtrader, offering flexibility for algorithm customization and deployment.
2. **Considerations When Choosing a Platform:**
    - **Programming Language Support:** Ensure the platform supports your preferred programming language (e.g., Python, C++) for coding algorithms.
    - **Backtesting and Simulation:** Evaluate the platform's capabilities for backtesting strategies using historical data and simulating trades under various market conditions.
    - **Execution Speed and Reliability:** Assess the platform's infrastructure for low-latency execution, reliability, and handling of high-frequency trading (HFT) strategies.
    - **Integration with Data Feeds:** Check compatibility with market data feeds, order execution APIs, and third-party tools for comprehensive trading operations.
    - **Regulatory Compliance:** Choose platforms compliant with relevant regulations and security standards to safeguard trading operations and client data.

Monitoring and Adjusting Algorithms:

1. **Real-Time Monitoring:**
    - **Performance Metrics:** Monitor key performance indicators (KPIs) such as P&L, Sharpe ratio, drawdown, and win rate to assess algorithm performance.
    - **Market Conditions:** Continuously monitor market conditions, news events, and economic indicators that may impact algorithm performance and market volatility.
    - **Risk Management:** Implement real-time risk management protocols, including stop-loss orders, position limits, and portfolio rebalancing rules, to mitigate potential losses.
2. **Adjustment and Optimization:**
    - **Iterative Testing:** Conduct ongoing testing and optimization of algorithms based on new data, changing market dynamics, and performance feedback.
    - **Parameter Tuning:** Adjust strategy parameters (e.g., thresholds, trading rules) based on backtesting results and real-time performance to enhance profitability and risk-adjusted returns.
    - **Adaptability:** Develop algorithms with adaptive capabilities to respond to evolving market conditions, incorporate new information, and adjust trading strategies accordingly.
3. **Documentation and Analysis:**
    - **Record Keeping:** Maintain detailed documentation of algorithmic strategies, including code revisions, parameter changes, and performance analysis for audit and compliance purposes.
    - **Performance Review:** Regularly review algorithm performance reports, conduct post-mortem analyses of trade outcomes, and identify areas for improvement or refinement.

- o **Feedback Loop:** Incorporate insights from performance analysis, market observations, and feedback from stakeholders (traders, analysts, developers) to optimize algorithmic trading strategies continuously.

Best Practices:

- **Testing in Simulated Environments:** Before deploying algorithms in live markets, thoroughly test strategies in simulated environments to validate performance and minimize potential risks.
- **Risk Mitigation Strategies:** Implement robust risk management protocols and contingency plans to handle unexpected market events and minimize potential losses.
- **Compliance and Security:** Ensure adherence to regulatory requirements and implement stringent security measures to protect algorithmic trading operations and sensitive data.

By carefully selecting a platform, actively monitoring algorithm performance, and continuously adjusting strategies based on market insights and performance metrics, traders can effectively implement and manage trading algorithms to achieve consistent and optimized trading outcomes in both Forex and cryptocurrency markets.

Chapter 12: Trading Psychology

12.1 Understanding Trading Psychology

Trading psychology plays a crucial role in the success and profitability of traders in financial markets. Here's an exploration of key aspects:

Emotions in Trading:

- **Fear and Greed:** Emotions like fear of losses or missing out (FOMO) and greed for profit can cloud judgment and lead to impulsive trading decisions.
- **Overconfidence:** Excessive confidence in a trading strategy or personal ability can lead to taking on excessive risks or ignoring warning signs.
- **Patience and Discipline:** Maintaining emotional balance, patience in waiting for favorable trade setups, and discipline in following trading plans are essential for consistent performance.
- **Psychological States:** Understanding how emotions fluctuate during trading, such as during winning streaks or losing streaks, helps in managing emotional responses effectively.

Common Psychological Pitfalls:

- **Loss Aversion:** The tendency to hold onto losing trades too long in the hope of a reversal, leading to larger losses.
- **Confirmation Bias:** Seeking out information that confirms existing beliefs about a trade, ignoring contradictory evidence.

- **Impulsiveness:** Acting on emotions or short-term market movements without a clear strategy or risk management plan.
- **Herd Mentality:** Following the crowd or popular sentiment without conducting independent analysis, leading to suboptimal trading decisions.
- **Regret Aversion:** Avoiding making necessary changes to a trading plan or strategy due to fear of regretting the outcome.

Strategies to Manage Trading Psychology:

- **Mindfulness and Awareness:** Develop self-awareness of emotional triggers and biases affecting trading decisions.
- **Risk Management:** Implement robust risk management techniques, including setting stop-loss orders, position sizing rules, and diversifying portfolios to minimize emotional impacts.
- **Trading Plan:** Create and adhere to a well-defined trading plan with clear entry/exit criteria, risk-reward ratios, and profit targets.
- **Journaling:** Maintain a trading journal to track trades, analyze performance, and reflect on emotional states during trading activities.
- **Education and Training:** Continuously educate oneself on trading strategies, market dynamics, and psychological principles to enhance decision-making skills.

Understanding and managing trading psychology is essential for traders to maintain consistency, avoid emotional biases, and make rational decisions based on objective analysis and disciplined execution. By developing psychological resilience and applying effective strategies, traders can navigate the complexities of financial markets with greater confidence and success.

12.2 Developing a Trading Mindset

Developing a strong trading mindset is essential for traders to navigate the ups and downs of financial markets effectively. Here's how to cultivate key aspects of a trading mindset:

Discipline and Patience:

- **Adherence to Trading Plan:** Develop and follow a well-defined trading plan with clear entry and exit criteria, risk management rules, and profit targets.
- **Consistency:** Stick to predetermined trading strategies and avoid making impulsive decisions based on emotions or short-term market fluctuations.
- **Patience in Waiting:** Exercise patience in waiting for high-probability trade setups aligned with your trading strategy, rather than chasing after every market opportunity.
- **Routine:** Establish a trading routine that includes regular market analysis, strategy evaluation, and review of trading performance to maintain discipline.

Managing Stress and Emotions:

- **Emotional Awareness:** Recognize and acknowledge emotional reactions such as fear, greed, or anxiety that may impact trading decisions.

- **Mindfulness Techniques:** Practice mindfulness techniques, such as deep breathing or meditation, to manage stress and maintain focus during volatile market conditions.
- **Risk Management:** Implement effective risk management strategies, including setting stop-loss orders, diversifying investments, and allocating capital wisely to reduce emotional responses to market fluctuations.
- **Healthy Lifestyle:** Maintain a balanced lifestyle with adequate sleep, exercise, and nutrition to support mental and emotional well-being, crucial for sustained trading success.

Developing Resilience:

- **Learn from Mistakes:** Embrace failures and losses as learning opportunities to refine trading strategies and improve decision-making processes over time.
- **Adaptability:** Stay adaptable and flexible in response to changing market conditions, adjusting strategies as needed while maintaining a consistent long-term approach.
- **Positive Self-Talk:** Cultivate a positive and constructive inner dialogue to build confidence in trading abilities and reinforce disciplined behavior during periods of uncertainty.

Continuous Improvement:

- **Education and Reflection:** Commit to ongoing education in trading strategies, market analysis techniques, and psychological principles to enhance trading skills and knowledge.
- **Journaling:** Maintain a trading journal to track trades, document trading decisions, and analyze performance, facilitating self-reflection and continuous improvement.
- **Seeking Mentorship:** Seek guidance from experienced traders or mentors to gain insights, receive feedback on trading strategies, and benefit from their expertise in managing trading psychology.

By developing discipline, patience, and effective stress management techniques, traders can cultivate a resilient trading mindset that supports consistent performance and long-term success in financial markets. Balancing technical skills with emotional intelligence is key to navigating the complexities and uncertainties of trading with confidence and composure.

12.3 Building a Trading Plan

Building a comprehensive trading plan is crucial for traders to define their goals, establish a clear strategy, and maintain discipline in executing trades. Here's a structured approach to creating and implementing a trading plan:

Setting Goals:

- **Define Objectives:** Clearly outline your financial goals, whether they involve capital growth, income generation, or risk management.

- **Quantifiable Targets:** Set specific, measurable goals, such as achieving a target annual return on investment (ROI) or increasing portfolio value by a certain percentage.
- **Time Horizon:** Determine your investment timeline and whether you are focused on short-term trading opportunities or long-term wealth accumulation.

Creating a Strategy:

- **Market Analysis:** Conduct thorough market analysis using fundamental and technical analysis techniques to identify potential trading opportunities.
- **Asset Selection:** Choose specific financial instruments or assets to trade based on your market analysis and risk tolerance.
- **Entry and Exit Criteria:** Define clear entry points (e.g., breakout levels, moving average crossovers) and exit strategies (e.g., profit targets, stop-loss orders) for each trade.
- **Risk Management:** Develop robust risk management rules, including position sizing, risk-reward ratios, and maximum exposure limits per trade or overall portfolio.
- **Trading Style:** Determine your preferred trading style, such as day trading, swing trading, or long-term investing (HODLing), aligned with your risk profile and financial goals.

Sticking to the Plan:

- **Discipline:** Adhere to your trading plan consistently, avoiding impulsive decisions or emotional reactions to market fluctuations.
- **Review and Adjustment:** Regularly review and evaluate the effectiveness of your trading plan based on performance metrics and market conditions.
- **Adaptability:** Stay adaptable and open to refining your strategy or adjusting parameters as needed in response to changing market dynamics or new information.
- **Documentation:** Maintain detailed records of your trades, including reasons for trade decisions, outcomes, and lessons learned, to facilitate ongoing evaluation and improvement.
- **Psychological Resilience:** Manage emotions and psychological biases effectively by maintaining a disciplined approach and focusing on long-term goals rather than short-term fluctuations.

Implementing the Plan:

- **Backtesting:** Test your trading plan using historical data to validate its feasibility and profitability under various market conditions.
- **Simulation:** Practice implementing your plan in simulated trading environments to gain experience and confidence before trading with real capital.
- **Execution:** Execute trades according to your plan, ensuring adherence to risk management rules and monitoring trade performance closely.

Continuous Improvement:

- **Learning and Development:** Continuously educate yourself on market trends, trading strategies, and risk management techniques to refine your skills and adapt to evolving market dynamics.
- **Feedback Loop:** Seek feedback from experienced traders, mentors, or peers to gain insights into improving your trading plan and strategy.
- **Adaptation:** Be willing to adapt and evolve your trading plan over time based on new insights, market experiences, and personal growth as a trader.

By setting clear goals, creating a well-defined strategy, and maintaining disciplined execution, traders can build a robust trading plan that enhances their ability to achieve consistent and profitable outcomes in financial markets. Regular evaluation, adjustment, and continuous improvement are key to adapting to market changes and optimizing trading performance over the long term.

Chapter 13: Risk Management and Trading Discipline

13.1 Importance of Risk Management

Risk management is paramount in trading to safeguard capital and maintain consistency in performance. Here's an exploration of its critical importance:

Protecting Capital:

- **Preservation of Funds:** The primary goal of risk management is to protect trading capital from significant losses, thereby ensuring sustainability and longevity in trading activities.
- **Capital Allocation:** Implementing proper risk management techniques allows traders to allocate capital wisely across multiple trades and assets, reducing the impact of individual losses on overall portfolio performance.
- **Risk-Reward Ratio:** By maintaining a favorable risk-reward ratio in trades (e.g., aiming for higher potential rewards compared to potential losses), traders minimize the impact of losing trades on overall profitability.

Consistency in Trading:

- **Stable Performance:** Effective risk management fosters consistency in trading performance by mitigating the adverse effects of market volatility, emotional biases, and unexpected events.
- **Emotional Control:** Structured risk management strategies help traders maintain emotional stability and discipline, reducing the likelihood of making impulsive or irrational trading decisions.
- **Long-Term Success:** Consistently applying risk management principles over time contributes to sustainable trading success, allowing traders to weather market fluctuations and achieve their financial objectives.

Key Risk Management Techniques:

- **Position Sizing:** Determine the appropriate size of each trade relative to your total capital, based on predefined risk tolerance and the probability of trade success.
- **Stop-Loss Orders:** Set automatic stop-loss orders at predetermined price levels to limit potential losses on trades and protect capital from significant downturns.
- **Diversification:** Spread risk across different asset classes, markets, or trading strategies to reduce overall portfolio risk and enhance resilience to adverse market conditions.
- **Risk Assessment:** Conduct thorough risk assessments before entering trades, considering factors such as market volatility, liquidity, and correlation with other positions.

Implementing Risk Management:

- **Pre-Trade Analysis:** Assess risk factors and potential outcomes before entering into any trade, ensuring alignment with your risk management strategy and trading plan.
- **Monitoring and Adjustment:** Regularly monitor trade positions, market conditions, and overall portfolio risk exposure, adjusting risk management measures as necessary to adapt to changing circumstances.
- **Documentation:** Maintain comprehensive records of trades, risk management decisions, and performance metrics to evaluate effectiveness and facilitate continuous improvement.
- **Education and Adaptation:** Continuously educate yourself on advanced risk management techniques, market dynamics, and emerging risks to enhance your ability to manage and mitigate potential losses effectively.

Conclusion: Effective risk management is foundational to successful trading, providing protection for capital, promoting consistency in performance, and fostering long-term profitability. By prioritizing risk management principles and integrating them into your trading strategy, you can navigate financial markets with greater confidence, resilience, and discipline, ultimately achieving your trading goals and objectives.

13.2 Risk Management Techniques

Effective risk management is essential in trading to mitigate potential losses and safeguard capital. Here are key risk management techniques that traders employ:

Position Sizing:

- **Definition:** Position sizing refers to determining the amount of capital to allocate to each trade based on risk tolerance and the probability of trade success.
- **Risk Per Trade:** Calculate the maximum amount of capital to risk on a single trade, typically expressed as a percentage of total trading capital (e.g., 1-2% per trade).
- **Formula:** Use the following formula to calculate position size based on risk percentage and stop-loss distance:

    Position Size=Risk per Trade/Stop-Loss Distance

- **Example:** If you have $10,000 in trading capital and set a maximum risk of 1% per trade with a stop-loss distance of 50 pips, the position size would be $200 (=$10,000 * 0.01 / 50).

Diversification:

- **Purpose:** Diversification involves spreading investment capital across different assets, markets, or trading strategies to reduce overall portfolio risk.
- **Asset Classes:** Allocate capital to diverse asset classes (e.g., stocks, bonds, commodities) to minimize exposure to individual market fluctuations.
- **Trading Strategies:** Employ multiple trading strategies with different risk-return profiles to balance potential gains and losses across various market conditions.
- **Benefits:** Diversification enhances portfolio resilience, mitigates the impact of specific asset underperformance, and improves risk-adjusted returns over time.

Using Stop-Loss Orders:

- **Definition:** A stop-loss order is a risk management tool that automatically triggers a market order to exit a trade at a predetermined price level, limiting potential losses.
- **Purpose:** Protect trading capital by defining an exit point in advance, thereby preventing emotions from influencing trade decisions during market volatility.
- **Types:**
    - **Fixed Stop-Loss:** Set a specific price level (e.g., $50 below entry price) where the stop-loss order is triggered.
    - **Trailing Stop-Loss:** Adjusts dynamically with the market price, moving in favor of profitable trades to lock in gains while limiting potential losses.
- **Implementation:** Place stop-loss orders immediately after entering a trade, adjusting based on market conditions, volatility, and the trade's risk profile.

Integration and Best Practices:

- **Combined Approach:** Implement multiple risk management techniques simultaneously to enhance overall risk mitigation and portfolio stability.
- **Consistency:** Maintain discipline in adhering to predetermined risk management rules and strategies, regardless of market conditions or emotional impulses.
- **Review and Adjust:** Regularly review and adjust position sizes, diversification strategies, and stop-loss levels based on evolving market dynamics, performance analysis, and risk assessment.
- **Continuous Improvement:** Continuously educate yourself on advanced risk management techniques, market trends, and risk factors to refine your approach and adapt to changing market conditions effectively.

By incorporating position sizing, diversification, and stop-loss orders into your trading strategy, you can effectively manage risk, protect capital, and enhance the consistency and profitability of your trading activities in dynamic financial markets.

13.3 Maintaining Trading Discipline

Maintaining trading discipline is crucial for traders to adhere to their trading plan consistently and avoid making impulsive decisions that can lead to losses. Here's how to foster and maintain trading discipline effectively:

Following the Trading Plan:

- **Clear Guidelines:** Develop a well-defined trading plan that outlines specific entry and exit criteria, risk management rules, and overall trading strategy.
- **Commitment:** Commit to following the trading plan meticulously, ensuring each trade is executed according to predetermined rules and guidelines.
- **Review and Update:** Regularly review and update the trading plan based on performance feedback, changing market conditions, and personal growth as a trader.
- **Documentation:** Maintain detailed records of trades, including reasons for trade decisions and outcomes, to evaluate adherence to the trading plan and identify areas for improvement.

Avoiding Impulsive Decisions:

- **Emotional Awareness:** Recognize emotional triggers such as fear, greed, or impatience that can lead to impulsive trading decisions.
- **Pause and Reflect:** Before entering or exiting a trade, take a moment to assess whether the decision aligns with your trading plan and risk management strategy.
- **Risk-Reward Assessment:** Evaluate the potential risk and reward of each trade objectively, ensuring that the trade meets your predefined criteria for risk tolerance and profit potential.
- **Stress Management:** Practice stress-reduction techniques such as deep breathing or mindfulness to maintain emotional stability and clarity during volatile market conditions.

Developing Discipline:

- **Consistency:** Cultivate a habit of consistency in executing trades based on your trading plan, regardless of market fluctuations or short-term outcomes.
- **Routine:** Establish a daily or weekly trading routine that includes market analysis, strategy evaluation, and performance review to reinforce disciplined behavior.
- **Peer Accountability:** Seek feedback and accountability from fellow traders, mentors, or trading communities to stay accountable and reinforce trading discipline.
- **Continuous Learning:** Stay informed about market trends, trading strategies, and psychological principles through ongoing education and professional development.

Overcoming Challenges:

- **Stick to the Plan:** Resist the temptation to deviate from your trading plan in response to emotional impulses or external market noise.
- **Learn from Mistakes:** Embrace failures and losses as opportunities for learning and improvement, rather than allowing them to undermine your confidence or discipline.
- **Adaptability:** Remain flexible in adapting your trading approach based on feedback, experience, and evolving market conditions, while maintaining core principles of discipline and risk management.

By prioritizing trading discipline, following a structured trading plan, and avoiding impulsive decisions, traders can enhance their ability to manage risk effectively, achieve consistent trading results, and progress towards their long-term financial goals in the dynamic and competitive world of financial markets.

Conclusion: Final Thoughts

In the fast-paced and dynamic world of financial markets, achieving sustained success as a trader requires a commitment to continuous learning, staying updated with market developments, and adapting to changing conditions. Here are some key final thoughts to consider:

The Importance of Continuous Learning:

- **Evolution of Knowledge:** Financial markets are constantly evolving, influenced by economic trends, geopolitical events, technological advancements, and regulatory changes. Continuous learning ensures traders remain informed about new strategies, tools, and market dynamics.
- **Skills Enhancement:** By expanding knowledge through courses, books, seminars, and interacting with experienced traders, individuals can refine their analytical skills, decision-making processes, and risk management techniques.

Staying Updated with Market Developments:

- **Information Accessibility:** Access to real-time news, economic data releases, and market analysis is critical for making informed trading decisions. Utilize financial news platforms, economic calendars, and social media to stay updated with relevant information.
- **Market Sentiment:** Understanding market sentiment—how investors perceive and react to news and events—can provide insights into potential market movements and opportunities. Stay attuned to shifts in sentiment to adjust trading strategies accordingly.

Adapting to Changing Market Conditions:

- **Flexibility in Strategy:** Market conditions can shift rapidly, influencing asset prices and trading patterns. Traders must be adaptable, ready to modify trading strategies, adjust risk management techniques, and capitalize on emerging opportunities.

- **Risk Management:** In volatile markets, effective risk management becomes even more crucial. Implementing stop-loss orders, diversifying portfolios, and maintaining disciplined trading practices help mitigate potential losses and protect capital.

Conclusion: Successful trading is not just about executing profitable trades—it's about cultivating a disciplined mindset, embracing continuous learning, and adapting to market dynamics. By prioritizing these principles, traders can navigate the complexities of financial markets with confidence, resilience, and a strategic approach towards achieving long-term financial goals.

Remember, trading is a journey of growth and development. Each trade and market experience offers lessons that contribute to refining skills and improving outcomes over time. Stay committed to your trading plan, manage risk effectively, and embrace opportunities for learning and adaptation to thrive in the ever-changing landscape of financial trading.

Resources for Further Learning

Expanding your knowledge and skills in trading requires continuous education and access to reliable resources. Here are some recommended resources across various formats:

Recommended Books:

- *Trading for a Living: Psychology, Trading Tactics, Money Management* by Dr. Alexander Elder
- *Technical Analysis of the Financial Markets: A Comprehensive Guide to Trading Methods and Applications* by John J. Murphy
- *Market Wizards: Interviews with Top Traders* by Jack D. Schwager
- *Reminiscences of a Stock Operator* by Edwin Lefèvre
- *The Intelligent Investor* by Benjamin Graham

Online Courses and Webinars:

- Coursera: Various courses on finance, trading, and economics from universities and institutions worldwide.
- Udemy: Offers a wide range of courses on trading strategies, technical analysis, and risk management.
- Khan Academy: Free courses covering financial markets, investment principles, and economic concepts.
- Investopedia Academy: Courses on trading, investing, technical analysis, and financial modeling.

Trading Communities and Forums:

- **Reddit:** Subreddits like r/Forex, r/StockMarket, and r/CryptoCurrency provide discussions, insights, and community feedback.
- **Forex Factory:** A popular forum for forex traders offering discussions, market news, and trading strategies.
- **Trade2Win:** A community forum covering various trading topics, strategies, and market analysis.
- **StockTwits:** A social media platform focused on stocks, providing real-time market insights and discussions.

Additional Resources:

- **Financial News Platforms:** Bloomberg, Reuters, CNBC provide up-to-date financial news, market analysis, and economic data.
- **Technical Analysis Tools:** TradingView, MetaTrader platforms offer charting tools, technical indicators, and analysis features.
- **Podcasts:** Listen to trading podcasts such as "Chat With Traders," "The Trading Lifestyle Podcast," and "The Investors Podcast" for insights from industry experts.

These resources offer a comprehensive foundation for traders at all levels, from beginners seeking basic knowledge to experienced traders looking to refine their strategies and stay updated with market developments. Continuously exploring new resources and engaging with trading communities can enhance your trading skills, decision-making processes, and overall success in financial markets.

Glossary of Terms

Key Forex Terms

- **Currency Pair:** A pair of currencies traded in forex markets, representing the exchange rate between the two currencies. Example: EUR/USD (Euro/US Dollar).
- **Exchange Rate:** The price of one currency in terms of another, determining how much of one currency is needed to purchase a unit of another currency.
- **Bid Price:** The price at which a trader can sell a currency pair.
- **Ask Price:** The price at which a trader can buy a currency pair.
- **Pips:** The smallest unit of price movement in a currency pair, typically equal to 0.0001 (except for Japanese Yen pairs, where it is 0.01).
- **Spread:** The difference between the bid and ask price of a currency pair, representing the transaction cost.
- **Leverage:** The ability to control a large position with a smaller amount of capital, amplifying potential profits and losses.
- **Margin:** The amount of money required to open and maintain a leveraged trading position.
- **Stop-Loss Order:** An order placed to automatically close a position at a predetermined price level to limit losses.
- **Take-Profit Order:** An order placed to automatically close a position at a predetermined price level to lock in profits.
- **Margin Call:** A notification from a broker requiring additional funds to be deposited into a trading account to maintain open positions due to insufficient margin.

Key Cryptocurrency Terms

- **Cryptocurrency:** A digital or virtual currency secured by cryptography, used for secure and decentralized financial transactions.
- **Blockchain:** A decentralized and distributed digital ledger technology used to record transactions across multiple computers, ensuring transparency and security.
- **Bitcoin (BTC):** The first and most well-known cryptocurrency, created by an anonymous person or group known as Satoshi Nakamoto in 2008.
- **Ethereum (ETH):** A decentralized platform that enables developers to build and deploy smart contracts and decentralized applications (DApps).
- **Altcoin:** Any cryptocurrency other than Bitcoin, often used to refer to alternative cryptocurrencies.
- **Wallet:** A digital storage solution for holding cryptocurrencies, allowing users to send, receive, and store their digital assets securely.
- **Mining:** The process of validating and adding new transactions to a blockchain, typically associated with proof-of-work cryptocurrencies like Bitcoin.
- **Fork:** A change or update to the underlying rules of a cryptocurrency protocol, resulting in two separate versions of the blockchain.
- **ICO (Initial Coin Offering):** A fundraising method for new cryptocurrency projects, where tokens are sold to early investors in exchange for funding.

Conclusion

This glossary provides a foundational understanding of key terms in both forex and cryptocurrency trading. Familiarizing yourself with these terms will help you navigate discussions, analyze market information, and make informed trading decisions in the dynamic world of financial markets and digital assets.

Useful Tools and Resources for Traders

Here is a list of websites and tools that can assist traders in their trading activities, market analysis, and staying informed:

1. **Trading Platforms:**
   - **MetaTrader 4 (MT4) and MetaTrader 5 (MT5):** Popular platforms for forex and CFD trading, offering advanced charting, technical analysis tools, and automated trading capabilities.
   - **TradingView:** A web-based platform for advanced charting, technical analysis, and social trading. It supports multiple asset classes including forex, stocks, cryptocurrencies, and more.
   - **Thinkorswim:** A trading platform by TD Ameritrade offering comprehensive tools for technical analysis, options trading, and paper trading.
2. **Financial News and Market Analysis:**
   - **Bloomberg:** Provides real-time financial news, market data, and analysis across global markets.
   - **Reuters:** Offers breaking news, economic data, and market analysis catering to financial professionals and traders.
   - **CNBC:** A leading financial news channel and website offering market updates, interviews, and analysis on global markets.
3. **Economic Data and Calendars:**
   - **Forex Factory:** Provides a comprehensive economic calendar, market news, and forums for forex traders.
   - **Investing.com:** Offers economic calendars, real-time quotes, and financial news covering global markets and asset classes.
4. **Cryptocurrency Exchanges:**
   - **Binance:** One of the largest cryptocurrency exchanges globally, offering a wide range of cryptocurrencies for trading.
   - **Coinbase:** A user-friendly platform for buying, selling, and storing cryptocurrencies like Bitcoin, Ethereum, and more.
   - **Kraken:** Known for its security and variety of cryptocurrency pairs, suitable for both beginners and advanced traders.
5. **Crypto Market Data and Analysis:**
   - **CoinMarketCap:** Provides cryptocurrency market data, including prices, market capitalization, trading volumes, and historical data for thousands of coins.
   - **CoinGecko:** Offers comprehensive cryptocurrency market data, charts, and analysis, including developer activity and community metrics.
6. **Educational Resources and Communities:**
   - **Investopedia:** Offers articles, tutorials, and educational content on finance, investing, trading strategies, and market concepts.
   - **Trading Community Forums:** Platforms like Reddit (r/Forex, r/CryptoCurrency), Forex Factory forums, and StockTwits provide discussions, insights, and community support for traders.
7. **Technical Analysis Tools:**

- o **TradingView:** Besides charting, it offers a wide range of technical analysis tools, indicators, and drawing tools for traders.
- o **MetaTrader Platforms:** MT4 and MT5 provide built-in technical indicators, custom indicators, and expert advisors (EAs) for automated trading strategies.
8. **Risk Management and Portfolio Tracking:**
    - o **Risk Management Tools:** Use position sizing calculators, stop-loss calculators, and risk management spreadsheets to manage and analyze risk in trading.
    - o **Portfolio Trackers:** Apps and websites like Blockfolio, Delta, and CoinStats help track cryptocurrency portfolios, monitor market prices, and analyze portfolio performance.

These tools and resources cater to traders of various experience levels, providing essential information, analysis tools, and platforms for executing trades across different financial markets and digital assets. Incorporating these resources into your trading routine can enhance decision-making, improve trading strategies, and keep you informed about market trends and developments.

Sample Forex Trading Plan

1. Market Analysis:

- **Technical Analysis:** Use of candlestick patterns, support and resistance levels, moving averages (e.g., 50-day, 200-day), and key indicators like RSI and MACD.
- **Fundamental Analysis:** Consideration of economic indicators (GDP, employment, inflation) and central bank policies affecting currency pairs.

2. Trading Strategy:

- **Timeframes:** Focus primarily on daily and 4-hour charts for trend identification and entry signals.
- **Entry Criteria:** Entry based on confirmed technical signals (breakouts, reversals) aligned with fundamental analysis.
- **Exit Criteria:** Set profit targets based on technical levels and trailing stop-loss to protect against adverse price movements.

3. Risk Management:

- **Position Size:** Calculate position size based on risk per trade (e.g., 1-2% of account balance).
- **Stop-Loss:** Place stop-loss orders based on technical support levels or maximum acceptable loss per trade.
- **Risk-Reward Ratio:** Aim for a minimum 1:2 risk-reward ratio on trades to ensure potential profits outweigh potential losses.

4. Trading Psychology:

- **Emotional Discipline:** Maintain discipline in executing trades according to plan, avoiding impulsive decisions driven by fear or greed.
- **Journaling:** Keep a trading journal to track trades, analyze performance, and identify areas for improvement in strategy execution.

Sample Cryptocurrency Trading Plan

1. Market Analysis:

- **Technical Analysis:** Use of cryptocurrency-specific chart patterns (e.g., bull flags, triangles), Fibonacci retracement levels, and key indicators like RSI and volume analysis.
- **Fundamental Analysis:** Evaluation of whitepapers, development team credibility, adoption rates, and regulatory developments impacting cryptocurrencies.

2. Trading Strategy:

- **Timeframes:** Utilize shorter timeframes (1-hour and 4-hour charts) for intraday trading or swing trading strategies.
- **Entry Criteria:** Enter positions based on confirmed technical signals (breakouts, trend reversals) supported by fundamental analysis of the cryptocurrency.
- **Exit Criteria:** Determine profit-taking levels based on technical resistance levels or trailing stop-loss to secure gains and manage risk.

3. Risk Management:

- **Position Size:** Calculate position size based on risk per trade (e.g., 1-3% of account balance) and the volatility of the cryptocurrency.
- **Stop-Loss:** Implement stop-loss orders based on technical levels or maximum acceptable loss per trade to protect against sudden price movements.
- **Diversification:** Spread investments across multiple cryptocurrencies to reduce overall risk exposure and enhance portfolio stability.

4. Trading Psychology:

- **Patience and Discipline:** Maintain patience during volatile market conditions, sticking to predefined trading rules and avoiding emotional trading decisions.
- **Continuous Learning:** Stay informed about new developments in the cryptocurrency market, adapt strategies based on market trends, and learn from both successes and failures.

These sample trading plans provide a structured framework for developing your own personalized trading strategies in Forex and cryptocurrency markets. Tailor these plans to suit your risk tolerance, trading style, and market conditions, while consistently evaluating and adjusting your approach to optimize trading performance over time.

www.ingramcontent.com/pod-product-compliance
Lightning Source LLC
Chambersburg PA
CBHW082240220526
45479CB00005B/1286